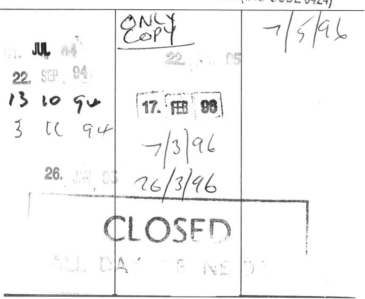

D. RAMON CABRERA

SPANISH TIGER

The Life and Times of Ramón Cabrera

Roy Heman Chant

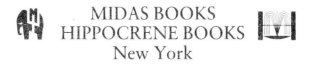

MIDAS BOOKS
HIPPOCRENE BOOKS
New York

Other military titles

Eighth Army Driver Maurice Merritt
The Bader Wing John Frayn Turner
For You the War is Over The Hon. Philip Kindersley
Prelude to Battle Gordon Moore
Stoker Greenwood's Navy Sydney Greenwood
So They Rode and Fought Major General S. Shahid Hamid
Marshal Ney Raymond Horricks
The Yanks Are Coming Edwin R. W. Hale & John Frayn Turner

First published in Great Britain in 1983 by
MIDAS BOOKS
12 Dene Way, Speldhurst
Tunbridge Wells, Kent TN3 0NX

ISBN 0 85936 087 3 (UK)

First published in USA by
HIPPOCRENE BOOKS INC.
171 Madison Avenue
New York, N.Y. 10016

ISBN 0–88254–883–2 (USA)

Printed and bound in Great Britain by
Robert Hartnoll Ltd, Bodmin, Cornwall.

Contents

To
Ivy and Adrian

The frontispiece portrait and the portraits and illustrations on pages 28, 41, 61, 81, 97, 100, 118, 120 and 159 are reproduced by courtesy of the British Library; those on pages 19, 67, 101 and 141 by courtesy of the Library of the Spanish Institute in London. The Cabrera coat-of-arms (p.161) and the hitherto unpublished photographs of the Count and Countess of Morella at Wentworth (pp. 134 and 135) are reproduced by kind permission of Doña Carlota Cabrera-Zanatti. The endpaper maps and the photographs on pages 130 and 151 are by the author.

Introduction

Ramón Cabrera, bandit leader, Carlist general, count, marquis, marshal, English country squire, whose remains lie buried in a quiet Surrey churchyard, was, to use the classic euphemism, a most singular man. He has attracted Spanish biographers, historians, novelists and poets through the years since his career began in the 1830s, and there have been one or two French and German works, but, as I discovered during research into his family life in England, no English book about him. There has been, it is true, the occasional chapter or reference by the mid-nineteenth century English traveller or military man in Spain and by later historians, but little else. Given his English associations, this surprised me. With surprise, however, went relief, for here was prime material – the rapscallion boy doted on by deeply religious parents misguided enough to train him for the Church; his novitiate escapades and pursuit of women, culminating in his bishop's refusal to ordain him; the failed priest turned barbaric butcher for Carlist Pretenders convinced of their divine right to the Spanish crown; the murders of the only women who had induced any spark of affection in him, one by his own hand in the terrible ferocity of revenge; the emergent general scoring great military success, only to encounter devastating defeat; the exile in France and England receiving a hero's welcome rather than a barbarian's scorn; his marriage to a remarkable English lady of great wealth; and his changing character under the influence of English life and thought . . . all against the backcloth of one of the most critical periods of Spain's turbulent history.

I first became acquainted with Cabrera when asked by a present-day connection if I could find out something of his English life and descendants. New material came to light, and the whole story led to deeper and deeper involvement until for these several years past Ramón Cabrera has lived with me. I am glad to get him out of my system. At the same time, it would be less than honest not to concede that, in following all the many changes in his character, personality and conduct, my own reactions and feelings changed too. First, horror and sheer incredulity; then contempt; on to a neutral acceptance; unexpected sympathy as the conscience of this unusual man was at last shown to be working, forcing him on to a courageous change of attitudes; and, finally, a sad emotion at his tomb as the biblical quotations around it drove home the lessons of man's everlasting folly.

This book does not set out to be a definitive life of Cabrera, which in any case would be an almost impossible task given the unreliability of all source material on the Carlist wars, with the victors invariably in control of the main channels of information. So it takes the broad picture, the highlights, avoiding nauseating repetition of bloody acts and tedious quotations from his correspondence with Carlist kings and conspirators, but at the same time taking in the intriguing, though not wholly irrelevant, digression and the amusing anecdote.

I am indebted to the Trustees of the British Library and to the Spanish Institute for permission to reproduce portraits and illustrations from their collections, as I am to their ever-helpful staffs. My personal thanks go to Don Pedro and Doña Carlota Zanatti-Cabrera, great-granddaughter of Marshal Cabrera, for access to family documents and paintings; to George Hills, biographer of Franco and author of other major works on Spain, for his expert counsel; José Manye, Spanish writer and broadcaster, for reading the typescript; Ron Davis, Virginia Water historian, for local information and for discovering rare photographs; but primarily to my longtime friends Don Fernando and Doña Rosa Omegna for first arousing my curiosity about Cabrera and then generously helping me in my task.

London 1983   *Roy Heman Chant*

1
The Boy

If you drive westwards out of London through Staines to Virginia Water and there take the turning opposite the Wheatsheaf Hotel, you will quickly come upon the pretty village church, its slender spire thrusting up through cloistering trees from sturdy clock-faced tower. In the far left corner of the churchyard, iron gates open on to railed-off square against the churchyard wall, mysterious in the tree-dimmed light, where a cross of polished granite rises proud and strong from four-tiered plinth, its grey-green sheen undimmed by time and storm. At the base, the stone is carved to show a warrior's helmet, sword, spear and shield, with a wreath of laurel. The inscription reads:

Ramón Cabrera,
Field Marshal in the Spanish Army,
Count de Morella,
Marquis del Ter. Born at Tortosa,
December 27, 1806.

In that year, George III, of the house of Hanover, was on the throne of England. Napoleon, having picked up with his sword the crown of France, was planning to filch for his brother Joseph the crown of Spain. In that much troubled land the Bourbon King Charles IV was moving towards abdication to make way for the French usurper, having already laid the foundation for a far longer and more cruel struggle than that arising from the Napoleonic invasion. He had secretly changed the Spanish law of succession, an act that was to cause Spaniard to fight Spaniard in one of the cruellest wars in history, to embroil the other two powers, and to carve out the life of the boy born on the banks of the river Ebro as the year 1806 was coming to its end.

As the nineteenth century opened one of Tortosa's better-known citizens was José Cabrera, captain of a river boat owned collectively by himself and a handful of other locals, in which he traded the twenty or so miles from Tortosa down to the mouth of the Ebro and along the Mediterranean coast. His wife, Maria, was from an equally well known local family named Griño, and two days after Christmas 1806, when she was twenty-three, Maria gave birth to a son in their little terraced cottage in one of the narrow streets near the ancient church of San Pedro. They called him Ramón.

From documents in the archives of Tortosa Cathedral, from Spanish biographers and historians of the period quoting anecdotes of local inhabitants recollected years later, it is possible to build up a picture of the Cabrera family and of Ramón's early life as he began his march into the history books and his longer journey to the mystery grave in an English village churchyard. The remembered tales are doubtless coloured in the light of the boy's development and the man's reputation and so should be taken with some reserve; but the overall picture is well defined. The family was deeply religious and much respected in the locality. Because of their close connection with the Church, and not because the infant was in any way frail, he was baptized on the day of his birth by visiting priests from the cathedral. The couple were delighted with their son, and his arrival was said to be the impetus for José's efforts to improve his lot. He bought a twenty-five ton *falucca*, the Mediterranean sailing barque, and became his own master. It was one of the biggest in the area, and not now having to share the profits with others he built up his business and added two smaller boats, using his little fleet in the profitable costal trade between Barcelona in the north and Valencia in the south, and doubtless in a bit of smuggling too.

Father and mother doted on their son, Maria's devotion being so intense as to draw the description 'near idolatry' from watchful neighbours. Ramón developed into a boy with incredible energy and courage, one who quickly got caught up in more than the normal boyish escapades. His animal spirits and the frequency with which he picked fights with other boys, and won them, earned him the nickname *El Batallador* at a very early age.

During this period, the War of Independence against the

French occupying forces, which had its beginnings in the historic *Dos de Mayo* rising in Madrid in 1808, was influencing the thoughts and actions of most Spanish families, whatever their class, and countless people everywhere were ready to sacrifice everything to get rid of the French. The Cabreras were among this group in Tortosa, and when French troops occupied the town they had to flee. José, Maria and the young Ramón got away with what they could, and took their boats down the Ebro and along the Valencia coast to the little port of Vinaroz. José worked up a new business, but his health broke down and he died there in 1812, with Ramón not yet six years old.

Maria was then twenty-nine, and the young widow found it increasingly difficult to control the aggressive tendencies of her growing son. Back in Tortosa, the French having left, he fought more and more, stoned the neighbours' windows as well as their more prized possession, their chickens, and organized gangs to smash the wares of hawkers who came to peddle the products of the Valencia potteries, bringing down a host of complaints on his mother's head. The neighbours could not understand how so devout and respected a woman could have so wild a son. With her savings running down and the boy so obviously needing the strong hand of a father, Maria decided to remarry. So on 25 September 1816, at the age of thirty-four and with Ramón nearly ten, she married another Tortosa boatowner, Felipe Calderó, a widower with one son.

The stepfather brought Ramón to heel a little, although it was clear that he, too, was very fond of the lad, who remained the spoiled favourite of the family. Felipe brought in one of the Church fathers to teach Ramón to read and write and to learn a bit of Latin, but he was an unwilling pupil. He was put to work in a local shop, but the young Cabrera was not for the restricted world of the counter; nor did he take kindly to the boat business.

When he was in his mid-teens a canonry became vacant in Tortosa Cathedral. The Cabreras, though only local tradespeople, believed they had a right, handed down from more affluent ancestors, to name the successor, so they tested their claim in the ecclesiastical court. In those days, even more than now, it was the great pride and one of the highest aspirations of Spanish families, particularly in the small towns and villages, to be able to point to one of their number as a member of the Church – still almost the only avenue through which a poor boy could break the chains of humble birth. It was probably this that made the Cabrera family go ahead, despite Ramón's obvious unsuitability.

The claim was presented by his uncle (a fisherman) and aunt. The learned fathers took three years to come to a decision, but in the end they upheld the claim, and granted Ramón a bursary, with all its rights and revenues. So at the late age of nineteen, and much against his own will, he went off to the local seminary to study philosophy and theology. He quickly built up a reputation, not for industrious study or piety, but for levity, disobedience and immorality. It is wrong to suggest that he did not have the intelligence to profit – he was too bright-witted for that. The truth was that his extrovert, rebellious character was diametrically opposed to the religious state, and any hopes that his misguided relatives had of changing him were quickly shattered.

He was among the first to mock the professors at lectures, and quickly became the leader of other rebellious students, whose amusements always had a flavour of violence. Ramón, impulsive and irrepressible, was ever in the vanguard, waving his tricorne novitiate's hat as he urged on the others in their many gang-fights with the local boys, which increasingly took on the form of organized battles. After one fight on a particularly hot and dusty day, Ramón jumped into the Ebro to cool off. He picked up some disease from the muddy waters and defied the diagnostic talents of the local doctors for two years. This was no sham; he became very ill and his devoted mother is given credit for saving his life: she sent him off to the more experienced medicos of Barcelona. After three months he came home cured.

Absence and illness had produced not the slightest difference in him; he returned as irresponsible as ever. So his parents reluctantly tried another move; they sent him into the seminary as a boarder. Again, the sedate atmosphere of the place failed to influence him. When the bells rang out at dead of night, shattering the peace of the reverend fathers in their cells and waking the slumbering populace outside, whose was the ghostly hand? When the friars found themselves locked out of their cells, who had hidden the keys? When the priestly stew was more than piping hot and the startled monks gasped for breath at the table, who had spiced the cooking pots? Ramón was the natural suspect, but no one could or would provide the evidence, and he himself was delighted to join in the subsequent investigations.

With the impunity he seemed to enjoy he became more and more audacious. He found new ways of creating upheavals in the pious atmosphere of the seminary. This type of behaviour was not uncommon among the student fraternity in Spain, but Ramón Cabrera carried it beyond the accepted limits. He took to getting out of the building at night. If he could not browbeat the porter into letting him throught the gates, he would climb over the walls. The municipal guards who patrolled the town at night were fair game for Cabrera and those students he induced to accompany him. Street lanterns were put out, balconies raided, their furnishings and flowers destroyed, and a peep taken behind the curtains. Ramón became the Notorious Student of Tortosa, completely fearless, but at the same time generous to a fault, lending money to less well-off colleagues as they required it.

Soon he was paying closer attention to the young ladies of the town than his nocturnal forays had hitherto allowed. As holder of a Church foundation, he was authorized to collect monies due to him under his bursary. This gave him access to the houses of some of the best families in the town, and the dovecotes fluttered as the daring and aggressive young man thrust his way into them. The señoritas responded, despondent señores erupted, and the threat of duels pervaded the air. Cabrera was always ready to throw down a challenge; but no one risked taking him on. His despairing rivals joined where they could not win, and became his reluctantly admiring followers. In contrast he was not loath to put on the dutiful face of his calling, for at mass and in feast day processions he displayed intense and devoted religious fervour, a contrast that drew further expressions of horror from the good people of Tortosa.

With all this, it is surprising to learn that Ramón actually took minor orders in the Church; but no surprise to find that when he presented himself for examination to show that he was fitted for the priesthood the Bishop of Tortosa, Dom Victor Sáez, refused to ordain him. A second time . . . and a third. Some said that this was because of his immorality in general and his pursuit of women in particular; others that he was too ignorant, a charge already disproved; more that his buccaneering spirit was so unacceptable that Bishop Sáez simply could not bring himself to ordain him. One suggestion, that the decision was motivated by Cabrera's exaggerated liberal ideas in a land of traditional absolutists, is utterly absurd, as his subsequent actions were to show. The bishop, in a classic understatement, said Ramón had no vocation for the Church, and told him he was more fitted to become a soldier. His opportunity was soon to come.

2
The Backcloth

When Charles IV changed the Spanish law of succession he did so by revoking the Salic Law, a law taken from the ancient Salian Franks and in France and some other European countries formulated into a statute barring women from succeeding to the throne, the aim being to prevent the union of two countries by the marriage of a king of one to a queen of another. The Salic Law had been introduced to Spain by the first Bourbon king, Philip V, specifically to ensure that there would be no such union between France and Spain. This was largely at the instigation of England, which wanted at all costs to avoid such an upset to the balance of power in Western Europe.

Charles IV was Philip's grandson, and his reasons for repealing the law and reinstating the right of female succession have puzzled many writers, since he already had sons. But it is clear that he did so because of a clause restricting succession to males born in Spain, which questioned his own position as king as he was born in Naples. He therefore abrogated the law *in toto* and chose not to publish the rescinding legislation, which was termed the Pragmatic Sanction, and which had been approved at a secret session of the Cortes, the Spanish parliament, in 1789.

There is no obscurity about the reasons that led Charles IV's son, Ferdinand, to make his father's act known when he became king. When the French invaded Spain in 1808, Charles IV abdicated in favour of Ferdinand. But Napoleon stepped in and summoned to France Charles and Ferdinand, and Charles' other sons Carlos and Francisco – in fact, the whole Spanish royal family – and kept them there. The French emperor then sent his brother Joseph to Madrid to pick up the Spanish crown. But Joseph ran into a hornet's nest of opposition, for exaggerated reports of the magnitude of the

Dos de Mayo rising had swept the country, crystallizing Spanish patriotism into a countrywide struggle to evict the French and bring back a Bourbon king. Though still in captivity in France, the hopes of the people of Spain were vested in Ferdinand, who became known as Ferdinand the Desired.

Six years were to pass in grim struggle before the War of Independence – the Peninsular War as the English know it – was won, and desire fulfilled, the French finally being driven out by the British forces under Wellington. In the spring of 1814 Ferdinand returned from France to be crowned King Ferdinand VII, though the triumphal and tumultuous welcome turned sour as it became clear that he would rule as a despotic, tyrannical monarch who would have no truck with liberal reforms.

Ferdinand was by then twenty-nine and without a queen. His wife Maria Antonia, a Neapolitan princess, had died eight years earlier – poisoned, according to one strong rumour, by her mother-in-law. In 1816, two years after his return, Ferdinand remarried; his bride was Princess Maria Isabella of Portugal. Within another two years he was widowed again, Maria Isabella dying in childbirth and the baby shortly afterwards.

In 1819 Ferdinand took as his third wife a Princess of Saxony, Maria Josefa Amelia. This marriage lasted longer, but gave Ferdinand little happiness, for her attachment to the church, the confessional and the rosary developed into an intense religious mania, and Ferdinand still had no heir when the Church enfolded her for ever in May 1829.

Ferdinand was by then fat and gouty and looked much older than his forty-four years. According to Richard Ford's *Gatherings from Spain* the king was rarely seen without a cigar, a very large thick Havana 'made expressly for his gracious use as he was too good a judge to smoke his own manufacture'. Even of these, said Ford, he seldom smoked half; the remainder was a grand perquisite. The cigar was one of his pledges of love and hatred. He would give one to his favourites when in sweet temper; and often, when meditating a treacherous coup, would dismiss the unsuspecting victim with a royal *puro*. When the happy individual got home to smoke it, he was saluted by a constable with the tyrant's order to quit Madrid in twenty-four hours.

Gout, cigars and premature age notwithstanding, soon after Maria Josefa's death Ferdinand intimated his desire to marry once more, and the court set to work. His youngest brother, Francisco de Paula, almost certainly fathered by his mother's lover, the Minister Godoy, rather than by Charles IV, was married to a formidable Neapolitan princess, Carlota, one of the host of daughters of King Francis I of Naples. Carlota seems to have been the chief schemer in the quest for a fourth wife for Ferdinand. What more natural than that she should look to one of her own unmarried sisters? So it was that the hothouse court of Naples again produced a bride. She was Maria Cristina, the second daughter of King Francis.

Twenty-three years old, lively and charming more than beautiful, she made a triumphal journey through Europe to Madrid. Until her arrival in Spain, Ferdinand had seen only a portrait of his bride-to-be. On seeing her in the flesh, winsomely dressed in blue, he was delighted and some of his youthful zest surged back into him. They were married in the Church of the Atocha in Madrid on 12 December 1829, the wedding coaches passing beneath banners and decorated arches as cannon boomed and trumpets blared.

On 10 October the following year Ferdinand was presented with his long-wanted heir. Six months earlier, yielding to pressure from Maria Cristina, almost as strong willed, it transpired, as her domineering sister, the King had unveiled his father's secret act. He told the surprised people of Spain, in public proclamations, that the Pragmatic Sanction of his father had restored the right of female succession. His brother Carlos, hitherto next in line of succession, was perhaps the most suprised of all. He said he had never heard of the Pragmatic Sanction and would have none of it. If Ferdinand died without a son then the throne was his by divine right. Don Carlos was never to waver in his belief that he was the chosen instrument of God, and he had many in his support, despite the argument of the King's men that female succession had been the tradition in Spain until Philip V altered it.

The precaution Maria Cristina had taken in getting the Pragmatic Sanction published was shown to be completely justified on that day in the royal palace in Madrid when she produced her first-born. It was a Sunday, and the corridors outside the Queen's apartments were thronged with courtiers as the doctors fussed around the royal bedside. They moved forward expectantly as the doors of the Queen's bedchamber opened and the newborn child was borne out on the traditional silver salver. King Ferdinand anxiously put the question that was in everyone's mind: 'What is it?' he asked. 'A robust infanta, your majesty.' The King tried hard to hide his disappointment, while friends of Don Carlos strove to suppress their sighs and smiles of relief. The child was christened Maria Isabel Luisa, but she was always known as Isabel.

Hopes that the claims of the Carlists, as the supporters of Don Carlos were called, might dissolve in the natural course of events were raised when Maria Cristina was seen to be pregnant again. But the medical–protocol scenes in the royal bedchamber were repeated almost precisely, for it was again a daughter, Luisa Fernanda.

This was the last chance, for Ferdinand became very ill – so ill that Maria Cristina sought advice of her ministers as to what she should do if the King died. After various suggestions – a joint regency among them – designed to placate Don Carlos, none of which Carlos would accept, the King's Minister of Justice, Francisco Calomarde, who may have been giving sincere advice but more probably was in the Carlist camp, persuaded Ferdinand that, unless he repealed the law of female succession, people would rally behind Don Carlos and there would be a bloody civil war. Convinced that he was dying, Ferdinand signed a decree repealing the Pragmatic Sanction. The decree was printed ready for publication and some Carlist supporters posted it up on hearing that the King was dead. They as quickly pulled it down again when the news proved to be premature.

Ferdinand suprised his doctors and everyone around him by recovering, and the decree was never published, though it had been printed. History gives prime credit for this to Carlota, ever watchful over the interests of her regal sister and the infant Isabel. The King had fallen ill at La Granja, the Spanish Versailles, some fifty miles out of Madrid. Carlota was at the

Cabrera's adversary, Maria Cristina de Bourbon, fourth wife of King Ferdinand VII. When he died she became Queen Regent for her infant daughter Isabel and secretly married a corporal of the Royal Bodyguard.

time in Cadiz, four hundred miles away. On hearing of the decree, she hurled herself back to Madrid, her coach covering the huge distance in less than two days, relays of horses speeding her way. Reputed to be capable of swearing like a carter, she stormed into the palace and berated all present. She ordered the president of the ancient Council of Castile to produce the decree, snatched the parchment out of his hands, and tore it into little pieces. She then turned on Calomarde and boxed his ears. The minister, more surprised perhaps than outraged, maintained his dignity and quietly replied: '¡Manos blancas no ofenden!'

Carlota's white hands may not have offended Calomarde, but time would soon show that they had woven a scarlet pattern of future bloodshed for Spain. Ferdinand dismissed Calomarde, who proceeded into exile, and then went farther than merely cancelling the decree which Carlota had so unconstitutionally torn up. He had already made a will bequeathing the crown to Isabel. Now he called together the Cortes in a ceremony of pomp and clamour in the ancient church of San Geronimo, and had its members swear allegiance to the Infanta Isabel as Princess of the Asturias, the direct heir to the throne. Don Carlos was not among them.

Ferdinand's recovery was short-lived. On 29 September 1833, two weeks before his forty-ninth birthday, at the royal palace in Madrid he had a stroke and was dead in five minutes. The Infanta Isabel, three years old, was immediately proclaimed Queen, with Maria Cristina, herself only twenty-seven, Queen Regent until her daughter came of age at eighteen.

King Ferdinand had often said: 'Spain is a bottle of beer and I am the cork. When that comes out, Spain will boil over.' As if to prove his point Don Carlos, who had been sent by Ferdinand to Portugal, immediately declared that he was the rightful successor, and proclaimed himself Carlos V, King of Spain. Northern Spain, stronghold of regional rights and privileges, was, except for the big towns, solidly for him; in the east, there was a similar though patchier situation. Abroad, he had the support, if not the overt recognition of Russia, Austria, and Prussia, who withdrew their representatives from Maria Cristina's court. The Pope sat on the fence; but France and

England formally recognized Isabel, who had immense followings in the towns and cities, and in many rural areas of the centre and south, and, of vital importance, the backing of the regular army and its generals.

Skirmishes between the army and armed supporters of Don Carlos had already broken out in several areas. And when Don Carlos issued from Portugal a general call to arms, after his sister-in-law the Queen Regent had outlawed him and confiscated his property, the cork was truly out of the bottle.

The support Don Carlos drew was nothing in the nature of adulation for him as an individual or as a ruler, although there were a few who were simply 'King's men'. The Church, which had long been prodding away at him to make some move, believing him to be a better Catholic than Ferdinand, backed him roundly, its fervour intensifying when the anti-clerical policy of the liberals, with whom Maria Cristina's regency was forced to associate for self-preservation, resulted in the wholesale confiscation of Church lands and some burning of churches and convents.

Allied to the priestly faction were regionalists interested mainly, if not exclusively, in retaining their local 'liberties'; traditionalists and other reactionaries; the inevitable courtiers, place-seekers and plain opportunists; and downright brigands simply out for plunder. All stood on the shoulders of a fervent, but not always ignorant, peasantry from which the Carlist chiefs recruited their common fighting men and on whom they relied for supplies and information. The Carlists saw themselves threatened with inundation by a slowly rising tide of liberalism and freemasonry, their conviction strengthened by the disturbing ideas then being canvassed on centralized government, the organization of the militia, total state control of education, and the separation of the throne from the altar. The freemasons in particular they regarded as atheists, and even devil worshippers, out to destroy Christianity in Spain, and they were convinced that all liberals were freemasons and all freemasons liberals.

There has always been a problem in writing about early liberalism in Spain. This had practically no connection with Liberalism as understood in England. When the word 'liberal' was first heard in Spain, it was used to bracket together those widely different sorts of people and bodies who separately or together opposed what they contemptuously called *serviles* (and not the least their masters), those whose views were still limited by the formula 'King and Church', and prepared to submit without question to the despotic rule of the Throne and a Church subservient to it. Although Western Liberalism took its name from the Spanish *liberales*, they themselves never got together to form a united front to pursue true Liberal political and economic doctrines, which were entirely incidental to the catalytic common bond – the destruction of the power of throne and altar.

The Carlists, in opposing the liberals, were wise enough to embrace from the outset the demands for the preservation of regional privileges, the *fueros*, thus ensuring the support of the Basques in the north and the Catalans in the east. And they went into battle under the banner 'God, Country, King' (but 'Country' in the limited sense of local autonomy), at one and the same time the champions of a Catholicism which wished to re-establish some sort of an idealized medieval state; of a monarchy that would be little short of despotic; and of such widespread regional autonomy as might only flow from the most advanced twentieth-century Liberal thinking. There had, however, long been pointers to a civil war between the 'two Spains' of so-called liberalism on the one hand and the forces of traditional reaction on the other. This would doubtless have come in any event; what Ferdinand's death and Don Carlos' claim to his throne did was to precipitate it.

Don Carlos could not immediately get back into Spain from Portugal for he was prevented from re-entering by Spanish government forces along the Portuguese border, so he got there by way of England. With William IV now on the throne and Palmerston at the Foreign Office, Britain had entered into an alliance with France, Spain and Portugal to maintain the thrones of the child queens Isabel in Spain and Maria in Portugal (also threatened, in a strangely similar situation, by a Pretender, Dom Miguel, her uncle and Don Carlos' nephew), so the British government was quite ready to help Don Carlos when he expressed a desire to go to England. Don Carlos, with his wife the Portuguese Princess Francisca, their three sons and a court of about fifty, were shipped out on the British man o'war *Donegal,* a vessel of seventy-four guns. When the ship arrived at Portsmouth in the middle of June 1834, Palmerston sent his under-secretary, Mr James Backhouse, to meet Don Carlos. The Spanish ambassador, the Marquis of Miraflores, also went to Portsmouth.

Backhouse tried to persuade Don Carlos to renounce his claim to his niece's throne and undertake not to return to Spain, and disclosed that he was empowered to offer him a Spanish government pension of £30,000 a year if he agreed to this. Don Carlos was unyielding. He spurned the offer and declared his unalterable belief that he was the legitimate monarch of Spain, and that Isabel and her mother the Queen Regent were the true rebels. He declined to receive the Marquis of Miraflores, saying he was not aware that he had any representative at the Court of St James.

Don Carlos and his family came on to London, where they were installed in Gloucester Lodge, Brompton, the old home of the former Prime Minister and Foreign Secretary George Canning. Don Carlos remained there for no more than a fortnight. Towards the end of June it was put about that he was ill and that his wife and sister-in-law, the Princess de Beira, were taking turns at his bedside. Then, with his moustache cut off and his hair dyed, he slipped away one night and was driven by coach to the south coast, where under a false name and forged passport he took a steamer to Dieppe. Then he went by coach to Paris and down to Bayonne. Eluding the French police, he picked up guides who took him over mountain paths to the border, and early in July crossed into Navarre, which to this day remains a Carlist stronghold. He left his wife, her sister and his three sons in England; he was never to see his wife again. In September of that same year, at the age of thirty-four, she died at Alverstoke Rectory near Portsmouth, where the family had taken up residence; she was buried at Gosport, the plaque on her tomb declaring her to be Queen of Spain.

3
Fighting Cleric

Ramón Cabrera was almost twenty-seven when Ferdinand VII died, and displayed no evident political leanings as he continued his way of life in Tortosa. Although he was to become fanatical in his conviction that Don Carlos was the rightful king of Spain, available information suggests that at this time he was completely indifferent. Some of the enemies he had inevitably made in Tortosa were among the early volunteers for the army of the Queen Regent – the Cristinos as they came to be called after her name – and it may have been that this alone was sufficient to ensure his support for the other side.

Chiefly because of his reputation and generally rebellious nature, fingers were pointed at Cabrera as a likely enemy of the establishment, and he was called to account for meetings which he had been holding at a church with which he was connected on the outskirts of the town. Rumour had it that they were attended by people believed to have Carlist sympathies. Cabrera failed to satisfy the governor, Brigadier Bretón, who then prohibited the gatherings. Cabrera obeyed the order overtly, but restarted the meetings in the seminary to which, as a minor cleric, he had access but which, being Church property, the civil and military authorities dared not enter. The meetings took on a more sinister character and persons known to be in touch with Carlist guerrilla chiefs outside the town attended and collections were taken presumably for the guerrilla bands.

The governor intervened again and admonished the rector for allowing the meetings to go on in his establishment, although the reverend gentleman probably knew little about them. As by that time whole areas in the mountains around Tortosa had declared in favour of Don Carlos, these meetings were taken very seriously by the town authorities, who feared a rising in Tortosa itself. They decided that about sixty people regarded as security risks should be expelled and sent to places where the Queen's rule was more secure. Among them was Cabrera, who was brought before Brigadier Bretón on 12 November 1833 and ordered to go to Barcelona. Cabrera promised to obey and left three days later with other expellees. But out of sight of Tortosa he announced that he was going to join the Carlists at Morella, turned about and set off in that direction. Two friends decided to go with him, one of them the cook at the Tortosa seminary where Cabrera had made such an impious reputation. It is probably an historical invention, but Cabrera is supposed to have said when making his break with the Barcelona-bound deportees: 'In a short time my name will ring around the world.' Invention or not, it was a true prophecy.

Morella was a fortress on top of a cliff, some fifty miles southwest of Tortosa, in the mountainous area astride the borders of Aragon and Valencia known as the Maestrazgo, its walled town rising up in a pyramid to the fortress castle at the top.

A month after the death of King Ferdinand a decree was issued over the signature of the Queen Regent ordering the disarming of the so-called Royalist Volunteers, comprising at least 100,000 men who had been enrolled by the parties of absolutism throughout Spain, ostensibly 'to guard the throne and altar against any new attempts of the liberals and infidels', but now seen as an incipient army for securing the succession of Don Carlos. It was after this decree that Don Carlos issued from Portugal his call to arms.

The Maestrazgo, with its natural fortifications and bases for raids into the surrounding provinces, offered a tempting sanctuary for those in the south and east who chose to defy the Queen's order and respond to the Pretender's call. Morella itself, dominating the whole range, could be near impregnable if its ramparts were properly manned. Enough men arrived with arms to make this a practical proposition, and a governing junta was set up there. It was headed by a Baron de Hervés, who early in November issued a proclamation in favour of Don Carlos. The baron, however, was not the first to do so. This distinction went to the chief of posts and telegraphs in a town midway between Madrid and the Portuguese border called, ironically enough, Talavera de la Reina. Early in

October, a few days after Ferdinand's death, the postmaster, Manuel Gonzalez, called out the local Royalist Volunteers, took over the town and proclaimed Don Carlos king of Spain. Both he and the baron were quickly caught and executed.

Morella, with which Cabrera's name was later to become associated for all time, was in a state of confusion when he and his two friends arrived after slipping across the Ebro at Tortosa. Some of the baron's men had gone out on a raid and had been defeated by a force sent out from Tortosa. In the confusion the three volunteers found it difficult to get any attention, but Cabrera persisted and he and his two friends were accepted by Baron de Hervés and his guerrilla chieftains.

At first Cabrera was no more or less conspicuous than other recruits; and at his first encounter with the Cristino enemy he was visibly terrified when he came under fire. He freely admitted this, and said it was because the whistle of the bullets was new to him. He overcame this fear and quickly became known for his coolness and daring – as collected yet audacious as he had been when leading his gangs in Tortosa. He soon caught the eye of the local Carlist chieftains, and with his aptitude for things military, which the bishop of Tortosa had so clearly recognized, he started clawing his way upwards through the ranks. Almost immediately he was a corporal, then a sergeant, and in little more than a month *subteniente*. Within another month, that is in January 1834, he became a full lieutenant; by the middle of the year, captain in command of his own small force, getting his first mention in the government's official gazette in Madrid. Before the year was out the fighting cleric had become a colonel.

A year or so of operations had, however, brought little overall success to the Carlists in the Maestrazgo. Brigadier Bretón himself was the first to show that Morella was not impregnable, for he sent out a force from Tortosa and quickly drove out the badly organized defenders to raise the banner of the young Queen Isabel over the fortress again.

Things were in fact going so badly that Cabrera, even then enough of a tactician to be disgusted at the lack of resistance put up at Morella, decided to risk a journey of some 200 miles, much of it through Cristino territory, to go and see Don Carlos in Navarre, near the French frontier.

Cabrera's 'King', Carlos V, utterly convinced of his constitutional and divine right to the throne of Spain.

Inevitably, as in anything Cabrera had done since he was a child, there was gossip and scandalmongering. The trip was intended to be secret. So it was insofar as Cabrera and an accompanying officer named Garcia had forged papers and assumed names and disguised themselves as muleteers to pass through unfriendly parts. But Cabrera took along a woman as guide, Maria la Albeitaresa, famed for her knowledge of the mountain paths of Aragon. She was forty, but the stories said this did not prevent the twenty-eight-year-old Cabrera having a turbulent love affair with her during their camping stops before she completed her task and left them within striking distance of Don Carlos' headquarters. They reached Navarre early in February 1835 after a hazardous journey that had taken thirteen days. Don Carlos received his fanatical supporter from Aragon at the little town of Zuñiga, near the border with the province of Alava.

Cabrera's motives in visiting Don Carlos are not clear. He let it be known that he was going to Navarre to seek direct backing, in the way of arms and money, for the guerrilla bands in Aragon. This was undoubtedly true, but there could have been an ulterior reason, perhaps one of the early examples of the personal jealousies and rivalries in the Carlist ranks generally that were to prove an almost continuous obstacle to the united prosecution of their struggle.

In control of the Maestrazgo forces, if any one person could be said to be in control of what at that time were really little more than bandit raiding groups, was a chieftain named Carnicer, to whom Don Carlos had recently given the rank of brigadier and had named *comandante general* of Aragon. It was Carnicer who had made Cabrera a colonel, and the newly promoted officer had gone right into the outskirts of Cristino-held Tortosa to recruit a battalion, with which he joined Carnicer in the field. He accompanied Carnicer on successful raids on Molina de Aragon and Caspe, two towns a hundred miles apart, and shared rich prizes. But when they ventured across the Ebro into Catalonia to attack Mayals they encountered disaster, then suffered a worse blow at Montalban, back in Aragon, where they were completely routed by the Cristino commander, General Valdés. Cabrera, whose own presumptions and want of experience had contributed to these disasters, managed to save himself and reappeared, but with his numbers much reduced. This force in turn was decimated, and he was left with scarcely a dozen men of his original battalion. He withdrew to the Maestrazgo to build up again and learn the lessons of defeat; he studied military organization and tactics under the guidance of a veteran officer, and read histories of Spanish wars of the past, paying particular attention to the use of cavalry.

There was no doubt that he was a born leader, and that he could inspire or induce unswerving devotion, for he had no difficulty in attracting recruits, and soon he had a new force of two or three thousand men. His troops, many of whom would serve under no other officer, were now calling him Don Ramón and he took on the airs and trappings of a leader, calling himself *comandante*. It was said that he was determined at all costs to take over control in the Maestrazgo.

Such was the situation at the time he decided to go to Navarre, and it has been suggested that the main purpose of his visit to Don Carlos was to get himself appointed in Carnicer's place by the simple formula of cleverly discrediting him, blaming him for the comparative failure of the Maestrazgo operations, and expounding his own plan for terrorizing the whole area into support of the Carlist campaign. There is nothing to prove this, and Major Francis Duncan in his book *The English in Spain* said the charge was utterly without foundation. Nevertheless, the sequence of events is peculiar, and it is reasonable to ponder why it was Cabrera who made the journey and not Carnicer.

Cabrera spent eight or nine days at the royal headquarters. First he saw Don Carlos' Minister of War, Count de Villemur, and then the Pretender himself, as well as senior members of his court. Although Cabrera seems to have been despised by the courtiers, for no other reason than a sneering contemplation of his lowly birth, he apparently made an impression on Don Carlos. Although he came away empty handed, developments were to follow that would give some sort of credence to the stories of his visit to Navarre.

Cabrera returned to the mountains of the Maestrazgo bearing a royal command for Carnicer to present himself in Navarre. Carnicer responded to Don Carlos' call, named Cabrera as his deputy during his absence, and set out on the road similarly disguised as a muleteer and accompanied by the same officer escort, but without the woman guide. With the clear implication of treachery on someone's part, the story goes that the Cristinos knew in advance the exact details and timing of Carnicer's route and how he would be dressed. Carnicer's party was stopped as it was crossing the bridge over the Ebro at Miranda, and Carnicer was shot a few hours later. The escorting officer was spared and subsequently exchanged. Not long afterwards Don Carlos named Cabrera *comandante general* of Carlist forces in Lower Aragon. Cabrera was in control of the Maestrazgo.

4
Tiger

Cabrera immediately set to work to build up into a cohesive force bound only to his leadership the scattered guerrilla groups now wandering in the mountains and led by independent brigand chieftains. He formed a select guard for his own use, and established a ruthless military police, *Miñones*, who carried out his execution orders and maintained discipline and obedience in his own ranks as well. Soon the strength of his force was up to 4000 men and several hundred cavalry, which he used to great advantage, profiting from the military tactics he had been taught and by the practical experience he was acquiring in the field. Frequently he would abandon the security of the Maestrazgo for long spells, and go down to face the troops who were hunting for him, waging vicious warfare on the Cristinos wherever they could be found in the surrounding provinces and pillaging towns and villages remaining loyal to the Queen or doing their best to preserve a careful neutrality. All these operations brought in food and booty, in the sharing out of which he was said to be absolutely scrupulous, his subordinates paying with their lives for the least defalcation. Looters, too, suffered similar short shrift. One of his sergeants found in possession of stolen goods was shot, despite the fact that he had recently been decorated. Cabrera had his troops march past the body and he told them: 'A few days ago this sergeant was awarded the Cross of San Fernando for bravery. Today he is shot as a thief. Look and learn.'

In his clashes with the enemy he usually got away with captured muskets and ammunition, more arms for more recruits, as well as Cristino uniforms that his tailors adapted for the use of his men when he did not want them for the purpose of disguise. If things went badly he would simply disappear into the hills with his raiders, only to reappear

31

twenty, fifty, or even a hundred miles further on. If they got worse, he would send his men to their homes 'to change their shirts', as he put it. Then as Cristino despatches were saying that the guerrillas had been defeated and dispersed, the so-called destroyed became the destroyers and more Cristino forts, troops, arms and ammunition fell to his surprise attacks.

Cabrera's military ability was becoming increasingly recognized; unfortunately his prowess was always accompanied by a terrible ferocity and his achievements tarnished by a frightful cruelty and vindictiveness. The analogy of the tiger emerging from its lair to maim and kill could not be avoided, and after the fighting cleric and the dashing lieutenant and colonel he became known, among his enemies at least, as the 'Tiger of the Maestrazgo'.

Cristino prisoners were slaughtered by the dozen, as were civilians who got in the way, or who were nothing more than unhelpful. Women, particularly the wives of Cristino officers, were taken hostage if the opportunity occurred, and he seduced them, in and out of captivity, with charm, or brutality where charm failed.

One of the more lurid stories about him was told by one of the English commissioners Palmerston sent out to Spain to report on the situation in the Queen's armies, and to do what he could to lessen suffering and maintain what humanities could be kept. Cabrera had billeted himself at the house of a friend, a staunch Carlist and a captain of Realistas (the disbanded Royalist Volunteers). He was attracted by his host's daughter and tried to seduce her. She repelled his advances and he threatened her, saying she had better be ready and willing the next time he came. The girl told her father, who at once sent her out of the town. When Cabrera turned up again he asked his friend what had become of his daughter; he merely replied that she had gone away. Cabrera made no comment on this at the time, but at dinner that night he told his host that he was wanted outside. The unsuspecting man went out and was seized by some of Cabrera's men at his own door and shot. Although the commissioner, Colonel Alderson of the Royal Engineers, could not have been a witness, he said the story came from personal knowledge and was 'a matter beyond dispute', giving the name of the victim as Monferrer and the place Villahermosa. And he added: 'Even savages respect the rites and debts of hospitality, but to murder a man whose only offence was saving his child from shame was a degree of brutality reserved for Cabrera.'

The east of Spain was not, of course, the only theatre of war. It was at that time a minor one compared with the north, where the Basque provinces and Navarre had been almost solid in their support for Don Carlos since the time of the death of Ferdinand; and where, within sixteen days of the king's death, there had been another execution to give added weight to the widely held contention that it was the Cristinos who started the barbarities. This was at Pamplona, in the heartland of Carlism, from which the former governor, General Santos Ladron, had been exiled to Valladolid for his 'royalist' leanings; he escaped and returned to Navarre to raise a force of 1000 men and pronounce for Don Carlos.

Government troops were sent against him and he was captured, brought back to Pamplona and shot in the moat of the city where he had been a most popular governor – an execution Cabrera was fond of instancing in the endless argument about who started it all; and one that in its backlash united the northern provinces in their hatred of the regency and had the immediate effect of drawing hundreds of recruits to the Carlist banner.

This was then taken up by a distinguished commander, Tomás Zumalacárregui, a regular soldier who had opted for the Carlist cause to become the greatest of all Carlist generals. The magic of his name was far greater than Cabrera's, and to his devoted followers he was simply 'Uncle Tomás'.

Although, like Cabrera and other generals on both sides, Zumalacárregui was guilty of cruelty and shot prisoners, which became the accepted custom in a war where quarter was rarely given, he conducted himself with greater dignity and waged a united and successful campaign despite the fact that 10,000 British volunteers and 4000 men of the French Foreign Legion were fighting on the Cristino side.

The British, recruited under an order in council suspending the act designed to prevent such foreign enlistment, were under the command of the Member of Parliament for Westminster, Colonel de Lacy Evans, who became General Evans in Spain and was knighted on his return to England. Their intervention led Don Carlos to issue at Durango a decree that any foreign troops taken prisoner would be shot out of hand, which they were. The Durango decree produced indignant feelings among the British officers of de Lacy Evans' force, and the Government in London conveyed a protest to Don Carlos, who promptly reissued the decree.

The Legion's officers were not quite sure how to handle the situation, fearful of its effect on the men. Some had the decree printed and posted up; others read it to their troops just as they were going into action. One of de Lacy Evans' senior officers, Colonel Charles Shaw, later General Shaw and, in civilian life, Sir Charles, took the latter course, and offered ten guineas to any man who could catch Don Carlos or any of his chief people, as 'he would not mind shooting them'.

Neither the British, who suffered dire casualties, more from sickness than in battle, nor the French, made a lot of difference to the campaign, although they did have some psychological effect in encouraging the Cristinos and dismaying the Carlists. Zumalacárregui, however, was not to have the charmed existence of Cabrera. The Carlists everywhere were very conscious of the value that would accrue to their cause, in the eyes of the world if not locally, if they could capture and hold a major city. In the north Bilbao, with its industries, harbours and access to the Bay of Biscay, was a natural temptress, although Zumalacárregui did not want to have anything to do with an assault on it; he thought it was too well defended. He yielded to the pressures of the Carlist court, however, and laid siege to the city in mid June 1833. While watching an action a day or two after operations had started he was hit in the leg by a musket ball. He was taken to a field hospital, where his surgeons decided against removing the lead. He was taken farther behind the lines, fever set in, and he died before the month was out, as bewildered and puzzled as others as to the manner of his dying: 'Is a man to die of a single ball?' he had asked as the seriousness of his condition became apparent.

With his death, the forces in the north began to splinter. Cabrera emerged as the most successful and notorious commander and became the centre of Carlist hopes and aspirations in the east.

Soon Cabrera was having his first clashes with the Queen's general in Lower Aragon, Austin Nogueras, whose bloody and horrible exchanges with Cabrera were to drive the Carlist chief's instinctive cruelty to incredible depths of ferocity and revenge. Cabrera, demonstrating his military dexterity and mobility, sent out strongly armed units to attack towns and villages one after another. From the south-western slopes of the Maestrazgo he overran part of the province of Cuenca and ran right up to the border of Castile. He plunged down into Valencia to attack Requena and other places. The Queen's men followed him ceaselessly, relieving him of some of his booty and driving him back into the mountains, but never able to hold him there. As his forces became stronger numerically and in arms, he became bolder, and decided to go for a more important town than he had so far attacked. He chose Segorbe, some thirty miles north of the city of Valencia, then a town of seven or eight thousand people, strongly garrisoned and with Nogueras nearby leading a flying column to head the Carlists off. Cabrera left a unit commanded by one of his favourite subordinates, Forcadell, to create a diversion for Nogueras, and entered Segorbe with his Tortosan battalion and forty horsemen. While his men collected the prizes – food, mules, horses and muskets – Cabrera went off to the episcopal palace to present his compliments to the bishop. He led his men out of the town as Nogueras moved in.

This seems to have been a relatively bloodless coup, but from most of these clashes erupted the inevitable charges and countercharges of cruelty and atrocity, Nogueras and other Cristino generals getting almost as bad a name as Cabrera. During one of the Carlist forays into Teruel province, the defenders of a small fort at Rubielos, mainly national guards but including a few regular soldiers, put up a brave and stubborn defence. Although heavily outnumbered, they only gave themselves up on receiving Cabrera's signed pledge that their lives would be spared and that they would retain their arms and uniforms. The survivors, sixty-five in number, then marched out and were escorted to a nearby plain. There Cabrera called a halt for a meal. He fed his prisoners as well, then formed up his infantry and cavalry around them. The prisoners were then ordered to strip and run for their lives, whereupon he set the encircling troops upon them to cut them to pieces with lance and bayonet. In September 1841, on the sixth anniversary of the outrage, when the war was over, the victims were disinterred and solemnly reburied in the town of Rubielos.

The temptation of sixty-five uniforms, of which he was always in need to clothe more of his ragged army, was obviously too much for Cabrera, and it was probably for these alone that the prisoners were murdered, seeing that the surrender document specifically mentioned clothing.

Another bloody act came when Cabrera led a force off the seaward side of the Maestrazgo right down to the Mediterranean coast to attack the fort of Alcanar, which guarded the beach and approaches to the port and natural harbour of San Carlos de la Rapita. Hearing of the attack, the national militia of the nearby fishing port of Vinaroz, comprising practically all the young men of the place where Cabrera had spent some of his boyhood, set off to help their neighbours. Cabrera got wind of their approach, and his men fell upon the advancing column and wiped it out without pity. The youth of Vinaroz having been eliminated, the fort of Alcanar held out for a day or so, but then capitulated, its defenders suffering a like fate.

These massacres, and other incidents which followed, demonstrated Cabrera's implacable hatred of all national guards, probably dating from his clashes with them as a renegade youth. Any who fell into his hands were immediately executed simply because they were wearing the militia uniform, even though some of them may have worn it against their own inclinations, as all males between the ages of eighteen and fifty were liable to service.

Cabrera's ferocity seemed to feed on itself; his grinding mind certainly needed no such grist as was supplied by the equally ferocious butcheries of Carlists such as the Barcelona massacre early in the following year. This great city was housing over a hundred Carlists taken prisoner in skirmishes with General Mina, captain-general of Catalonia. On 4 January 1836 a mob ran through the streets shouting 'Death to the Carlists!' and demanding that all prisoners be handed over to them. Among the howling mob were uniformed members of the National Guard (or militia as it was more popularly known from an earlier title). Some of them were carrying new muskets supplied from HMS *Rodney* in Barcelona harbour under Britain's treaty with Queen Cristina's government. The acting governor of the city tried to dissuade the mob, promising that the Carlist prisoners would be tried immediately and just punishment meted out. The mob would not listen, and the governor had to give way. The rioters rushed to the citadel, where sixty-seven prisoners were held, and put scaling ladders against the walls. Some three hundred Cristino infantrymen stationed at the citadel did nothing to stop them; on the contrary, they helped the ringleaders to put up the ladders and climb over. Once inside they demanded of the commanding officer a complete list of all Carlist prisoners held in the city, which he gave to them. Then the Carlists in the citadel were led out one by one, 'with diabolical regularity' as one eyewitness put it, muskets placed at their heads, and shot.

The first out was a Carlist cavalry officer, Colonel Juan O'Donnell, member of a well-known Spanish family of Irish descent that had brothers fighting on opposite sides in this war. After he was shot, some of the ringleaders tied ropes to his body, threw it over the walls and dragged it through the streets, the crowds following in their thousands. In the square outside the theatre a great fire had been started; O'Donnell's head was hacked off and the body thrown on the fire, while the mob kicked the head through the streets as if it were a football. Ten officers and fifty-seven men were murdered at the citadel. The grisly scenes were repeated at two other prisons; even sick and wounded were taken from their beds and shot. Those who did not succumb to the first bullet were bayoneted to death; the grim total was 107 officers and men.

The touchpaper for this rampage had been equally barbarous actions by Carlist bands in the neighbourhood. General Mina had been harassing the Carlists, and a few days earlier a largish group in retreat had taken over a fortified castle, carrying with them over a hundred prisoners, mostly inhabitants of Barcelona. When Mina laid siege to the castle the Carlists threw their prisoners over the ramparts, firing at them as they crashed to their deaths on the rocks below. As if this was not enough to set the Barcelona mob alight, at about the same time another Carlist band had raided the mail to Madrid, killing most of the escort of national guards and regular troops.

The captain-general returned to Barcelona to discover that vengeance had been taken out of his hands. But soon he was playing a part, with his fellow commander in Aragon, Nogueras, in the dreadful event that was to drive the ferocious Cabrera to new depths of cruelty and revenge, and to send waves of nausea and indignation rolling round the world.

5

The Great Crime

One morning the following month the people of Tortosa were presented with the spectacle of soldiers marching an elderly woman through the streets, her hands clutching a crucifix to her breast as her trembling feet stumbled through the dust. At the Barbican she was blindfolded and left praying on her knees as a squad of eight Cristino soldiers armed with muskets formed up a few paces away, four in front, the other four in reserve behind them. The squad commander signalled with his sword, the men in the front row levelled their guns and fired, and the praying woman fell dead, shattered by four musket balls. Her name was Maria Griño. Her crime, simply being the mother of Cabrera.

In the middle of 1835 General Nogueras had ordered the imprisonment of Cabrera's mother, who was still living in Tortosa with her three daughters. Her second husband, Felipe, with his son, had followed his stepson Cabrera into the mountains. It was alleged that Maria was a Carlist conspirator, but this will not stand scrutiny, and it is clear that she was taken as a hostage with the hope that this would, perhaps, put some sort of restraint on her son's acts.

Early in February 1836 Cabrera put to death the *alcaldes*, or mayors, of two places in Lower Aragon, the villages of Torrecilla and Valdealgorfa. Mayors throughout Spain were the traditional provisioning agents for the Spanish armies. Cabrera shot these two on the grounds that they were Cristino spies and had supplied information about his troop movements, although doubtless he had in mind that it would deter village leaders from co-operating with Government forces. General Nogueras, as an immediate reprisal, and, as he put it, the better to serve the Queen, ordered the governor of Tortosa to take Cabrera's mother out of confinement and shoot her. The governor, not the one of Cabrera's student days but a new man, Brigadier Gaspar Blanco, and one of the few to show a breath of sanity and humanity in this ghastly episode, refused to comply and appealed to Nogueras' superior officer, the captain-general of Catalonia, General Mina.

Mina backed Nogueras and directed that the order should be carried out forthwith. At ten o'clock in the morning on Tuesday 16 February 1836 soldiers marched to the prison where Maria Griño was held. They allowed a priest to hear her confession, but she was refused holy communion and she was not permitted to see her children; nor was she accorded the dignity of a mantilla, so she walked bareheaded between the soldiers in their stovepipe hats as they escorted her to the place of execution. Her last words were: 'Tell my son not to take vengeance.'

Cabrera's activities had aroused such widespread terror that many Spaniards applauded the execution, until the consequences began to make themselves felt. It was four days before the news of his mother's death was broken to Cabrera, who was then at Valderrobres, one of the seats of the medieval kings of Aragon on the northern edge of the Maestrazgo some twenty-five miles from Tortosa. His aides had known about it the day after the execution, but they were afraid to tell him, although he had questioned them about the cause of their gloom. At length one of his favourite officers, Lieutenant Pertegaz, took it upon himself to break the news, and saw Cabrera at eight a.m. on 20 February in his billet in Valderrobres. After several minutes of cautious and hesitant exchanges, Pertegaz managed to blurt out the terrible news. Cabrera at first would not believe it, telling Pertegaz that he was delirious and to go away. Then, when convinced it was true, he went into alternate bouts of weeping and frenzied raging, tearing his hair, first saying that he wished to die, then that he would live to wreak vengeance, screaming abuse at Nogueras and vowing a war to the death with him even if it meant chasing him into the bowels of the earth.

When he had recovered his self-control he issued an order to his troops to go out into the surrounding countryside and exterminate all Cristino families, adding the biblical phrase 'unto the fourth generation'. He withdrew it, but then dictated a new order for the immediate execution of thirty people.

Murder in the Barbican . . . Cabrera's mother is shot.

Cabrera had also taken women hostages, and he had four of them in his hands at that moment, wives or daughters of Cristino officers. He had been convinced that while he held them no harm would have come to his mother. They were the wife of a colonel named Fontiveros, who had been commandant of the town of Chelva in Valencia when Cabrera attacked it six months or so before, Mariana Guardia, Francisca Urquesa and Cinta Fos. The order specifically named these four women. They were taken out and shot.

The execution of Cinta Fos, a pretty and vivacious girl of only nineteen who would sing and play the guitar for the troops at camp stops, made even Cabrera's closest associates gasp at his vicious impartiality. For Cinta was his sweetheart. Although held hostage, she had fallen in love with the dark-eyed Carlist chief, a dashing figure, despite a lack of inches, in his uniform of a white cape over dark blue coat and white

THE EXECUTION ORDER

Circular of the comandante-general of Lower Aragon:

The military governor of Tortosa, in a despatch of the 15th inst., states to me as follows: 'Immediately on the receipt of your despatch of the 8th inst. I communicated it to the captain-general of the army and principality because I did not think myself empowered to make the mother of the rebel leader Cabrera expiate the atrocities committed by her son, but at this moment I have received the post from Catalonia, with a despatch of his excellency for you, as also one for myself, in which he is pleased to tell me that your wishes are to be complied with; by virtue of which, tomorrow morning at ten o'clock the mother of the cruel Cabrera will be shot, and his three sisters taken up this night, although two of them are married to two National Guards of the marine in this place; and I have to inform you that I shall take up the near relatives of the other chiefs and self-styled officers, for the purpose of restraining these barbarians by putting some measure to their excesses. The executions to take place in the open space of the Barbican as being the public spot on which all those who may deserve it shall be shot; and I shall issue a circular to the towns of this district, for the information of the people and the terror of such of the evil-minded as may commit attempts on the lives of the loyal inhabitants. All which I hereby make known to the end that all the inhabitants of these districts may be certain that the barbarous Cabrera's lust for innocent blood has been the cause of the death of his mother, and will be that of his sisters if he persists in his atrocities; as such will be that of the wives, sisters, and mothers of the chiefs who are in my custody and who I shall order to be shot, five for each whom he shall assassinate. God preserve you many years.

Fresneda, 15 February 1836   Augustin Nogueras

CABRERA'S REPLY

The barbarous and sanguinary D. Austin Nogueras, who styles himself comandante-general of Lower Aragon, has just published as an act of heroism the atrocious assassination which, at his request, was effected in Tortosa on my innocent and unfortunate mother, who was inhumanly shot on the morning of the 16th inst. in the place of the Barbican, and my three sisters seized prisoner although two of them are wives of Nationals in that town. Horror-struck, and yet full of calmness and valour at this melancholy as well as cowardly and evil act, suited solely to men who seek to procure triumph of the cause they have embraced by infamous acts of terror, while plunging the country and families into sorrow and general mourning, and yet supposing that their enlightened conduct will be enough to serve the criminal usurpation which has produced so many victims, I, in the use of my powers which law and justice confer on my character of commander-in-chief of this province, named by the King and legal sovereign Don Carlos V, have in conference with his royal instructions issued the following regulations:

1. The self-styled Brigadier D. Austin Nogueras and all those whosoever are actually serving in the army or employed by the government of the queen called regent are hereby declared traitors.

2. All the individuals aforesaid, who may be taken, shall be shot by virtue of the above order.

3. These shall be shot immediately, as a just retribution for the assassination of my innocent mother: The lady of the Colonel Manuel Fontiveros, comandante that was of arms in Chelva, kingdom of Valencia, and who has been in my custody in order to restrain the range of the cruel revolutionists. As also three others, who are Cinta Fos, Mariana Guardia and Francisca Urquesa, and even to the number of thirty, which I mark down to expiate the infamous punishment of the best of mothers.

4. With a heart wrung with grief and eyes overflowing with tears while dictating this tremendous measure, I cannot do less than announce with sorrow that I not only disregard altogether the atrocities which cover me with mourning and affliction, but that their bloodthirstiness shall be revenged without fail, for each victim by twenty of the families of the assassins who shall continue them.

Valderrobres, 20 February 1836   Ramón Cabrera trousers, with red or white *boina* (the military beret), his black hair and full moustache glamorizing the outfit. She and her captor were often seen riding together, and it was rumoured that they were about to marry; yet on that vengeful morning, Cabrera had her executed with the others.

Some early books on Cabrera, and even standard reference works more than a hundred years later, say flatly that Nogueras then shot Cabrera's three sisters. It is true that they were 'taken up', as Nogueras put it in his execution order, and that he did threaten to kill them, but the threat was not carried out and they lived to join Cabrera on his marches. One died of typhus during the siege of Morella, but two were still alive fifty years later when the English lady who became Cabrera's wife named them as beneficiaries in her will. The Cabrera literature, too, shows a confusing inconsistency over his mother's age when she was executed. Most writers put it between sixty and seventy, one that she was seventy-two, blind and lame. Where no figure is essayed, she is invariably referred to as 'aged'. She was, in fact, fifty-three and in reasonable health.

It is not difficult to understand the terrible vindictiveness of her son's revenge. Apologists for him will say that his barbaric cruelty began here, but it is clear that this was the intensification of a pattern, not a new one, for it has been calculated, on the basis of documented testimony, that he had slaughtered at least two hundred prisoners and civilians in cold blood before his mother was shot. His jungle title wasn't enough now. Other titles were hung on him: barbarian, murderer, bandit; perhaps the most telling of all the simplest, the cruel Cabrera.

Nogueras called him, among other epithets, barbarian, and threatened to shoot five hostages for each person he shot. Cabrera, master of one-upmanship in words as well as corpses, replied with bloody barbarian, and said he would shoot twenty Cristinos for every one of Nogueras' victims. Nogueras achieved nothing for the Cristinos except his own removal from command and the legacy of increasing barbarity. Mina, his superior, stayed on; he offered his resignation but it was not accepted. Later, he was to plead that he had so much to occupy him in the field he had sanctioned the application from Nogueras as a matter of routine, without enquiring into it.

6
The Times Thunders

Revulsion at this extraordinary act by the Queen Regent's generals was expressed in most of the articulate capitals of the world, not least in Madrid itself. One newspaper in Maria Cristina's capital said: 'In the name of the holy cause of liberty, which we defend, in the name of humanity impiously outraged, in the name of civilization in every country, in the name, in fine, of heaven and earth, we from the bottom of our hearts raise a fearful cry of horror, of execration, and of reprobation against such unheard-of reprisals which, as we hear, have been perpetuated in the case of this sexagenarian mother, thus doubly miserable from the nefarious activities committed by her son, a spurious Spaniard, an apostate clergyman, and the chief of a gang of bandits.'

In other European cities pity for the mother made many people forget the son's crimes and begin to see him as an injured victim rather than a barbaric butcher. From London, *The Times* thundered out in a leading article which demanded disgrace and punishment for Nogueras, the executioner, and Mina, the overlord, and took in the Irish Rebellion, the French Revolution, and the troubles in Spain in one large canvas. As a prime example of the art of the essayist-propagandist of the 1830s it will bear quotation.

'It is doubtful whether modern history – and we will allow it to embrace 1000 years – offers any series of atrocities so revolting as those which during the present civil war in the Peninsula have disgraced the Spanish name and nation,' said *The Times*. 'The crueties perpetrated by the guerrillas during the war of what was called emancipation were indeed sufficiently barbarous, but being provoked in some measure by the sanguinary butcheries at Madrid and elsewhere, of which some of the French invading troops had been guilty, and being moreover exercised in favour of that quarrel which England herself had embarked in, this nation may not have been too curious in examining the details or very severe in judging them.'

Then to make the point for a question, the leader-writer sketched in with lurid strokes the horrors of the Irish Rebellion of 1798 and of the French Revolution nine years earlier, when, as he put it, 'French society, in an hour of perfect frenzy, presented nothing but the saturnalia of a band of lunatics and all semblances or pretence of regular government was wholly at an end . . . while in Ireland, Protestants, men, women and children, were by hundreds deliberately consumed to ashes in fiendish holocausts; and British ignorance, impelled by superstition, fanaticism, vague hatred and wild revenge shed blood, inflicted agony, and dealt out murder with a mingled sense of duty and enjoyment – all examples of human nature in the depths of moral decomposition.

'But what can excuse, or what account for, the crimes of these Spanish barbarians?' the question went. 'The war is doubtless a civil war; but it is one carried on by "regular governments" on both sides. There is no palliation from feverish and momentary rage, from the reckless violence of an infatuated rabble, or from the persecuting frenzy of superstition. All is sober, legalised bloodthirstiness. Carlos began by proclaiming that all constitutional prisoners should be put to death. Instead of forcing this despot, by a milder and more generous treatment of his own partisans, to renounce through shame such systematic barbarity towards his foes, the Queen's Government accepted the challenge and butchered the Carlist prisoners in return.

'The circumstance, however, which above all others has aroused the slumbering instincts of humanity in relation to this dismal contest is new, we hope and trust, even in Spanish annals,' *The Times* continued. Then, somewhat understating the case, it went on: 'Cabrera, a partisan of Don Carlos, has gathered some desperadoes about him and is accused, we dare say with some justice, of having committed many atrocities. What then is the result? It would have been quite fair to offer a large price for the capture of the barbarian who had violated the laws of war, had taken advantage of the confusion everywhere to perpetrate crimes which are equally incompatible with the usages of war and peace. Any punishment inflicted on such a criminal, after full proof of the identity of his person and of the reality of his offences, would have needed no justification. The Queen's General does not attempt to lay hold of the culprit in his own person; he hunts out a vicarious sacrifice and wreaks his vengeance on Cabrera's helpless and inoffensive *mother*!!'

The Times concluded: 'If we could indulge any hope of redemption for Spain, it would be founded on the evidence which has reached us of the thrill of disgust and horror produced at Madrid by this execrable assassination. The last accounts state that General Nogueras had issued the order under which this unhappy victim perished, after obtaining the sanction of Mina as Captain-General of the province. If this be so it mainly imports the honour of the Queen's Government, and the eternal cause of humanity, that the principal murderer, as well as the inferior general, should be disgraced and signally punished. It is dreadful to contemplate our King of England as the ally of a Government under which such iniquities can be practised. It is most painful to see our brave countrymen associated, though ever so indirectly, with cruelties so base and monstrous.'

The jibe in the last paragraph of *The Times* leading article was directed at the treaty under which the Whig government was supplying arms and ammunition to Maria Cristina's forces, and to the arrangement whereby British volunteers were fighting for her.

7

The Lords Fume

On the same day that *The Times* printed its editorial, the execution was raised in Parliament, where speakers in the Lords described it as monstrous, atrocious, disgusting. The Tory Opposition challenged the Government on the same points made by *The Times*, particularly the suspension of the Foreign Enlistment Act which had allowed volunteers to be legally recruited for the Cristino cause. The Lords debate is worth looking at, if not for the flowery oratory of that time, then for the personalities involved: Palmerston, Britain's imperious Foreign Secretary; the popular Lord Melbourne, Whig Prime Minister, who was to gain the affection of the young Queen Victoria as he guided the headstrong and inexperienced girl into her duties as a sovereign; Aberdeen, former Foreign Minister who was to become Prime Minister when the Crimean War broke out and lose office because of it; and Wellington, whose own accomplishments on the bloody battlefields of Spain had consolidated his military career and founded his political one – he had already been Prime Minister and Foreign Secretary.

The debate was opened by the Earl of Aberdeen, as opposition spokesman on foreign affairs, who felt that Britain was substantially participating in a cause and in a system of warfare which had been disgraced by atrocities and abominations unheard of in the history of any civilized country. The contest, from its very beginning, had been carried on under circumstances of peculiar ferocity. They had gone on increasing day by day until they had arrived at the very acme of ferocity and horror. When he used that phrase he was of course referring to the murder of that unfortunate woman, the mother of Cabrera. 'Now I really do not know that I have ever met with anything quite so monstrous, quite so atrocious as this murder,' said Lord Aberdeen. 'I do not believe that in the wildest excesses of the French Revolution anything so disgustingly horrible could be found.'

For this was not the act of the moment, he went on; this was not the offspring of a sudden and wild revenge, created by feelings springing from a sense of immediate injury – no, it was an act sanctioned by the highest authority in the country, that authority having had time for deliberate consideration. The government had entered into a treaty to supply the Queen of Spain with arms, ammunition and warlike stores of every description – a greater number of arms, Lord Aberdeen remarked, than the Queen of Spain had troops. It could never be supposed, by any possible understanding, that these arms and supplies were intended for any other purpose except the carrying out of legitimate warfare. Otherwise the government placed itself in some measure responsible for the conduct of those who used them.

But government ministers were further responsible. Under their advice, England had sent out a body of adventurers to take part in this contest. By their suspension of the law prohibiting the enlistment of men for foreign service they had virtually – he would say expressly – connected themselves with that service. The government had no right or reason to facilitate the enterprise of these persons in a foreign country. And Lord Aberdeen wanted to know what the government were doing to improve and soften, to modify and humanize, the character of this unholy and horrible war? If the government were prepared to declare that they would withdraw their subjects from Spain, and that no supplies should be furnished except for legitimate warfare, and not for the purpose of a war of tigers and hyenas, would not the Spanish government yield to the British government's wishes? If the barbarous nature of the parties concerned made this impossible, nothing could possibly justify support of such a contest for one moment longer. Lord Aberdeen moved that copies of correspondence between the government and the British ambassador in Madrid, together with the remonstrances addressed to the Queen of Spain on the subject, should be laid before the House.

The Prime Minister, Viscount Melbourne, began his reply by saying that he entirely and heartily agreed with all the sentiments of abhorrence which had been expressed, and he assured the House that nothing he might say was intended to show an inclination to palliate or excuse in any way the manner in which the war had unfortunately been carried on. The noble earl had said that the system now pursued was unparalleled. He would justly observe that contests of this kind were always carried on with the utmost bitterness of hostility; and, nodding across to the Duke of Wellington, he said he would refer to that war in which the noble duke opposite him had so greatly and honourably distinguished himself, and would say that it was disgraced by the most sanguinary and ferocious cruelty. He would say no more, lest it be supposed he wished to soften the feelings of detestation which their lordships so strongly and so properly entertained.

The government, the Prime Minister said, had not allowed the execution to pass in silence. Mr Villiers [ambassador in Madrid] had not waited to receive instructions, but had at once waited on the Prime Minister of Spain [the liberal, Juan Mendizábal] and insisted that the most proper inquiry should be set afoot. And the moment the news had been received in London, Lord Palmerston wrote to the Spanish Prime Minister expressing the utmost indignation and also demanding the most prompt inquiry and satisfaction. The consequence was that General Nogueras was deprived of his command and an inquiry ordered into his conduct. Ministers, Lord Melbourne went on, had done everything in their power to smooth and soften the system of warfare in Spain; but he could not agree that because they could not effect their wishes to the utmost extent they should sacrifice the great interests belonging to this question, that they should therefore throw up their views and change their policy towards the western part of Europe. He certainly was not prepared to go to that length, even on account of the continuance of those atrocities.

He would, however, again express the deepest horror and detestation of those atrocious acts and he could assure the House that he would do everything in his power to prevent them. He therefore readily acceded to the opposition motion. The papers might not be so full or so numerous as their lorships might expect, but he could confidently state that no opportunity had been lost to interfere generally on this point as a matter of principle, and to interfere singly on every new case or occurrence of this disgraceful kind which came to the notice of ministers. He would trouble their lordships no further, but merely express his confident belief that they were all most anxious to preserve the rights, the independence and the freedom of Spain.

The Duke of Wellington rose to say that expressions of discouragement and disapprobation, however strongly made, were not enough. The government had been placed in a very awkward situation. Nothing could be more evident than the government's loss of moral influence. By sending troops to Spain, Britain had not only invalidated that convention safeguarding prisoners on both sides which he himself had been instrumental in securing [the Eliot Convention]; it had made His Majesty a party to the war there, and thus lost all influence over Don Carlos, as well as the power of doing anything towards humanizing the war or effecting any useful purpose. The British troops, said the victor of Waterloo, had not been of the slightest use; on the contrary, because of their despatch, the government had lost its respect, its neutrality and the influence it might have exercised over the councils of the two belligerent parties.

So long as the British government kept a body of troops in Spain they would make no progress towards peace, do nothing towards a diminution of those atrocities, and day by day matters in Spain would become worse.

The Lords agreed to the opposition motion, but the documents laid before the House added little to what was publicly known or to what had been disclosed in the debate.

There were similar expressions of concern and distaste in the French National Assembly; and in the Cortes the anti-liberal factions used the occasion to make Mendizábal's already difficult position still more difficult.

Before the end of 1836, Mendizábal, a Jewish businessman since described as Spain's first modern statesman, who two years earlier had been called home from a long exile in London to be first Finance Minister and then Prime Minister, was forced out of office by other problems. Nevertheless, he continued to play a most important part in government affairs, for his successors did their best to carry on his policies, whose main planks were the reconciliation of the political parties so that business activity could be increased and public credit re-established, while at the same time bringing the war to a successful conclusion without further taxation. Convinced that to defeat the Carlists a fully trained army of 100,000 men was needed, Mendizábal had floated a loan on the London market in his efforts to find the money; while at home he had been the prime mover in the wholesale confiscation of Church lands and property. But in spite of dribbling the huge quantities onto the market, he failed to get fair prices. The London loan, too, was not a success, so that at times some of the officers and men in the new army received no pay, and disaffection was rife.

8

Vengeance is Mine

Vengeance is in my heart, death in my hand,
Blood and revenge are hammering in my head.
(Shakespeare: *Titus Andronicus*)

Cabrera's thirst for reprisals, and Cristino acts of counter-reprisal, led to a period of horror and desolation unequalled in all the Carlist wars. Cabrera issued Nogueras with a challenge for a duel, alone, with conditions according to the Cristino general's choosing. Nogueras, removed from his command but still fighting in the field, chose to ignore it. There were bloody deeds of revenge by the Carlists almost immediately, notably at Chiva, in Valencia, and at Cherta, near Tortosa. Among the hated national guards taken prisoner here, according to a short Spanish history of Cabrera published soon after the war, was the husband of one of his sisters from Tortosa, and the Carlist chief ordered his execution with the others. Despite the conveyed entreaties of the entire family, he would not alter his decision. At the last moment, however, the condemned man's young son, Cabrera's nephew, was brought to the scene, and his presence alone stopped Cabrera from executing his brother-in-law.

It was one of the rare occasions when the Carlist leader showed any mercy at all, if one excepts a later event at San Mateo when he intervened to stop his troops bayoneting to death Cristino prisoners. This was not right, he said; they should be shot, and he promptly saw to it that the survivors were so despatched.

Cabrera had set up his headquarters in the walled town of Cantavieja, on the western side of the Maestrazgo. He beat the Cristinos to this strategically important place by acting instantly on information received. He had been operating in the Chiva area, near the city of Valencia (where he had suffered one of his rare defeats), when he heard that the Cristinos were proposing to fortify Cantavieja and make it one of their centres of operations against him. Cabrera immediately dispersed his troops, after arranging a later rendezvous, and with a couple of officers and half a dozen men rode quickly back to the Maestrazgo. With the help of Carlist prisoners inside, he made sure that if anyone was going to fortify Cantavieja it was he. Not only did it become his fighting and administrative head-quarters, but also his arsenal and supply depot. He established foundries for making muskets and cannon, a gunpowder plant, factories to turn out uniforms and footwear for his growing body of troops, and of no less importance, a hospital for the wounded, and a printing press. He collected tolls from towns and villages over a wide area, and appointed a minister of finance to see that each enterprise received its proper share.

Cristino towns and villages in the plains and valleys for hundreds of miles around felt the bite of this organized backing for Cabrera's operation, and the Cristino generals showed new respect for him in the way that they redeployed their forces and in some cases avoided risky actions with his troops.

A year before, soon after Cabrera had taken over from Carnicer, Nogueras had paid him a rare compliment. In a message to the captain-general of Valencia after an action at Alloza when, with 1500 infantry and 150 horsemen, he had failed to pin down Cabrera's very much smaller force, Nogueras said he had never seen such decision and cool courage. Even the troops of Napoleon could not have carried out a retreat in such good order; he warned his superior officer that if Cabrera's wings were not clipped he would give the Cristinos a lot of trouble. So far, no one had succeeded in clipping them, and soon Nogueras was to witness another example of the Napoleonic touch. Meanwhile, events were to take Cabrera down into Andalucia and to great successes there, albeit at great cost to his position in the Maestrazgo.

In Navarre, the Carlist court was split by dissension. Don Carlos, now aged forty-eight, diffident in his approach to military matters if resolute in his belief that he was the legitimate king, was scarcely master in his own camp. Urged on by ambitious generals and pushed and pulled by place-seeking courtiers, he frequently escaped their pressures, and his own decisions, by long recourse to prayer. A pained, tired expression usually on his long, moustachioed face, sad of eye and cold in manner, he never looked a king and seldom acted like one. Now the so-called moderates on the one hand, who eventually might have achieved some sort of compromise on his claim, and the absolutists on the other, were often more concerned in prosecuting their place-seeking intrigues and even personal vendettas than in closing their ranks in the overall interest of the Carlist campaign.

Much the same sort of thing, of course, could be said about the court in Madrid where, as much as anywhere else, the blood and anarchy foretold by Ferdinand could plainly be seen. Around the Queen Regent and the young Queen Isabel were politicians of more varied hue than there could ever be at the court of Don Carlos; the politicians, the place-seekers, the generals who preferred the tactics of palace intrigue to the strategy of the battlefront. All these and, one would hope, some sincere men, were surrounded in the outfield by bankers and speculators, more interested in the commission they might get in raising loans for quickly changing regimes than in stability of government.

A searching comment on this instability was made by the Revd Thomas Farr, in his book *A Traveller's Rambling Reminiscences of the Spanish War*, written at that time. 'I see no end to this war,' he wrote. 'Buy not into the Spanish Funds [then on offer in London]. A friend of mine used to sum up the value of the securities of that Government in a few words: It is against their principle to pay the interest and it is against their interest to pay the principal!'

Out of the confusion of the Carlist court in Navarre there did, however, emerge one positive policy, mistaken though it proved to be. A majority of Don Carlos' advisers, misled, perhaps, by the popular support the Carlists received from the peasantry of the north, became convinced that it was necessary only to show the Carlist flag in other parts of Spain for the crown to come tumbling on to Don Carlos' head. From this idea stemmed the great Carlist marches, culminating in the Royal Expedition, the incredible march on Madrid.

The first foray was made by Batanero, one of the many fighting priests in the Carlist armies, who, at the head of 250 cavalrymen, arrived within striking distance of Madrid. His excursion caused great alarm in the capital, but it had insufficient strength and no backing to pose a serious threat, and Batanero returned to Navarre with loot and little else.

Next, two experienced generals, Basilio Garcia and Juan Balmaseda, led a much stronger expedition on a similar route into Old Castile, ending up, as Batanero had done, near La Granja. It was the summer of 1836 and the royal family were at the royal palace there to escape the heat of Madrid. Balmaseda concocted a plan to kidnap Maria Cristina and her two daughters. Garcia would not go along with it, and they returned without this royal prize, and without having stirred up the people, though laden with other spoils and bringing back a number of recruits for the Carlist armies.

Then came a brilliant display of military skills by the man who had been Zumalacárregui's chief of staff, General Gomez. With five infantry battalions, two squadrons of cavalry and a brace of cannon, something like five thousand men in all, this forty-year-old general marched right across northern Spain, taking Oviedo, capital of the Asturias, and the great religious shrine of Santiago de Compostela, almost on the Galician shore of the Atlantic, cleverly keeping ahead of the pursuing army of the Queen's General Espartero, while defeating lesser Cristino generals. Having traversed the country east to west, he then crossed it north to south, first of all making a long thrust east of Madrid, routing a division protecting the capital and capturing its commander, General Lopez, and on almost to the outskirts of Valencia. Then he went across southern Spain to the Mediterranean near Gibraltar, before turning north and striking a direct route back to his starting point near Bilbao, utterly indifferent, so it seemed, to Cristino columns moving on either side of him or popping up in his path. He reached his home base a week before Christmas 1836, six months and 2500 miles after starting out, his sheer audacity contributing to his success.

In Andalucia Gomez had been joined by Cabrera and his staff and a few cavalry. Their joint military operations were a success – among the prizes the great city of Cordoba with 2500 prisoners, 4000 muskets, and £200,000 worth of booty – but the leadership combination was not. The swashbuckling and ferocious Cabrera, as in the past, could not get on with the polished professional soldier. He was irritated by the contemptuous manner of Gomez, who treated him as an inferior and, crowning insult, declined to mention him in despatches. Cabrera then became so troublesome that Gomez contemplated having him shot as a mutineer against his authority. To avoid this, Gomez insisted that they part.

Cabrera and his cavalry went off into La Mancha, where he subdued several Cristino garrisons and reinforced his own strength, but having already made up his mind to go back to Navarre and apprise Don Carlos of his troubles with Gomez. At about the same time he received information that the Cristino army of the centre was threatening Cantavieja, his headquarters. Whether he intended to do anything about this soon became academic, for before November was out he learned that it had fallen. He speeded up his march towards Navarre, shedding some of his units, but this time he did not quite get there. He and a cavalry escort had almost reached the Ebro opposite Navarre when they ran into a strong Cristino force under General Iribarren, in the province of Soria. Cabrera took avoiding action, but ran into his pursuers on a particularly black night, receiving bayonet and sabre slashes in the back and leg. He crept into a wood, where he was found by one of his officers. He took Cabrera back to Almazán, where the parish priest, Manuel Maria Morón, gave him sanctuary, concealing him in his house.

The priest's secret leaked out, whereupon the mayor announced that he would organize a thorough search the next day. That night some friends of Cabrera forced a local peasant to deliver a message to the mayor. When he opened it, he found it was signed by Cabrera. It was the kind of message he often sent out when his troops were on the march and living off the countryside; it ordered the mayor and population, on pain of death, to provide several thousand rations, but it purported to come from a village a few miles away. The mayor did not stop to obey. With the local militia and regular troops, he immediately decamped, fully expecting the tiger to pounce at any moment, leaving the way clear for Cabrera to be moved to a place of safety. He recovered, but abandoned his intention of going to Navarre; he turned about and made his way back to Lower Aragon. There, at Mora de Rubielos, he was reunited with his reassembled forces, amid scenes of great emotion, which he fanned into enthusiastic battle cries as he swore to recapture Cantavieja. But within a matter of days he was wounded again.

Marching towards Torreblanca on the Mediterranean coast near the end of January 1837, Cabrera encountered a Cristino force led by General Borso, who immediately attacked. When Cabrera saw his men falling back, he led a cavalry charge into the fray in an effort to retrieve the position. They ran into a volley of fire and Cabrera was knocked off his horse, hit by a musket ball. His troops thought he was dead and retreated in confusion. Cabrera was taken on a stretcher to the caves of Vinroma, where his medicos recovered the bullet and treated his old wounds, which had opened up. Nothing daunted, Cabrera continued to direct operations from his sickbed and was soon defying his doctors' orders and up and about again.

It was not long before he was tempted anew by the rich pickings to be had in the plains of Valencia. Cabrera's own sufferings had done nothing to temper his ferocity and soon new and bloody butcheries were being pinned to his name. One of his forces under Forcadell, then a colonel, routed a Cristino brigade at Buñol, killing 700 men and taking 320 prisoners, if the account is believed – casualty claims on both sides were always suspect, and in the end exceeded the total number of troops engaged throughout the whole period of the war. According to the custom, Forcadell had twenty-three officers among the prisoners shot.

About a month later Cabrera was well enough to rejoin the fray, his white cape and white horse again taunting the now cautious Cristino generals. Some Cristino troops and cavalry, probably the remnants of those mauled by Forcadell, had been resting and regrouping in Liria, and had now received orders to move to the security of Valencia fifteen miles away. Spies informed Cabrera of their intended move, and he waited for the right time and place, and falling upon the column on the outskirts of Burjasot he captured it, scarcely one soldier escaping. The prisoners numbered 727 and, as Forcadell had

The Burjasot fiesta – macabre massacre or anti-Cabrera propaganda?

done, and he himself had done so many times before, Cabrera had all the officers and sergeants shot.

Just outside Burjasot a little hill rose up from the plain, and from it could be seen the spires and houses of Valencia. Here, according to Cristino accounts, Cabrera established his camp, and a feast was prepared to celebrate the victory as well as the birthday of Don Carlos, which happened to coincide with it.

A table loaded with food and wine was set up in the open away from the tents, and Cabrera and his officers ate, drank and sang, while some sort of orchestra played. As the wine took its effect, Cabrera is said to have given orders for the officers and sergeants to be brought out and, during the drunken orgy, they were shot or bayoneted as the feast continued.

So goes the story, which has been accepted by some Spanish writers and by artists who saw enough in it to sketch impressions of the massacre, but vigorously rejected by others.

Cabrera said this was another of the inventions circulated by the Government side in order to discredit him. But by his own despatch at the time, and from remarks he made long afterwards, there is no doubt that prisoners were shot, although he disputed the circumstances.

In France years later, Cabrera spoke about the Burjasot killings, as well as the shooting of Cinta Fos and the other women hostages at Valderrobres. 'The memory of these ladies,' he said, 'will haunt me until I die.' But Burjasot he sought to justify, and in some detail. 'The order being given to shoot the officers and sergeants,' he said, 'many people from Burjasot and the neighbouring area crowded around, some to congratulate me on my victory, others out of curiosity. Sympathizers were making music and the peasants brought wine, water and food. I ate a little and drank a glass of water. I do not remember if there was sugar in it or a little wine, it being the case that I scarcely tasted it as my physicians would not allow it because of my wounds.

'The officers and sergeants were shot, as was the practice, and then my enemies deduced all those things they have said of me. This is the same thing as when a judge goes to a theatre or some other entertainment while a prisoner he has sentenced is awaiting execution. Nevertheless, nobody accuses the judge or calls him cruel. Between the theatre and a military camp there is a great difference. I am called a tiger and an executioner. With much more reason would a judge be called these things in the said case. I shot, being within my rights, but without the complacency and demonstration attributed to me. It was a war to the death and the prisoners were prisoners without conditions. And so all the officers, sergeants and soldiers could have been shot, but I resisted in making so much Spanish blood flow. Would you have me disobey the orders of my superior officers and keep them all prisoners when the Cristinos killed mine? And my mother? Had they pity for my innocent mother and the Carlist prisoners in Barcelona and the sick burned alive; the wounded of Cantavieja, throats slit in their beds; and all those individuals of my army who fell into enemy hands?'

Whatever one may think of Cabrera, or of the bestialities perpetrated by both sides in this unpleasant war, his logic as expressed here is irrefutable.

9

The Royal Expedition

These atrocious stories horrified public opinion everywhere, but perhaps more outside Spain than within. They seemed, however, to have no effect on Don Carlos, at least as far as Cabrera was concerned, for he showed increasing confidence in him; he had already named him *mariscal de campo* – in effect, field commander of the Carlists in Aragon – for his destruction of a Cristino division at Ulldecona, close to Tortosa. And when Don Carlos launched his great march on Madrid, he invited Cabrera to join it, and the Tortosan leader's contribution was to take his standing with the Pretender to its highest peak, and even, against their inclinations, impress his courtiers. But before this, Cabrera achieved his avowed aim of reconquering Cantavieja.

Five or six hundred of his men, under one of his experienced deputies Cabañero, a name that was to loom darkly in the Cabrera story, and another force under Forcadell, were laying simultaneous siege to Cantavieja and to San Mateo, thirty miles away on the coastal side of the Maestrazgo. Cabrera himself was holding a watching brief somewhere between the two places, and was in something of a quandary. The new Cristino commander of the centre, General Oráa, was hurrying up from Valencia with a lot of men. Should Cabrera drop the siege of one in favour of the other; if so, which? His dilemma was resolved for him, for before Oráa posed a direct threat Cabrera received news that Cantavieja was back in his hands. Civilian partisans inside the town were largely responsible for this; they helped Cabañero to enter, take the garrison prisoner, and use the fortress' own guns to subdue all resistance and ensure surrender. It was a comparatively bloodless affair; not so at San Mateo, to which Cabrera was now able to bring fresh reinforcements and apply full pressure. The defenders, waiting in vain for relief, put up a heroic resistance for four or five days before giving in, although here again treachery, or cowardice, decided the outcome. The officer in charge of one of the defending batteries, with his gunners, dropped a rope over the walls, slid down and went over to the Carlist lines. Cabrera immediately saw his chance and sent a group of his own men up the rope . . . and it was all over. This was the action that followed by the bayoneting of officers and militiamen prisoners in ditches outside San Mateo while the main body of the victorious troops celebrated mass in the town square, and by Cabrera's countermanding of this form of execution, only to order that the survivors be shot.

With Cantavieja back in his hands, refortified and provisioned to his liking, its foundries and factories extended, and more artillery at his command, Cabrera was again lord of the Maestrazgo, menacing huge areas of Aragon, Catalonia, and the rich plains of Valencia. Not complete master, however, for Morella, the great fortress dominating the range, was still in Cristino hands, and it was there that Oráa took his troops after reaching the San Mateo area too late. This did not stop Cabrera from dreaming and scheming for this great prize. He had spies and a small number of troops watching every movement, and at one time the fifth column which seemed to be operating inside most Cristino-held places in the area almost succeeded in handing over to Cabrera Morella as well; but the plot was discovered by the governor, who had all the conspirators executed. So when the Royal Expedition approached the Ebro towards the end of June 1837, Cabrera had to go off, leaving the coveted fortress still in Cristino hands.

The Royal Expedition was so called because Don Carlos himself headed it, and took along his whole court and all his advisers and hangers on, as well as an army of some fourteen thousand men. They formed sixteen infantry battalions, ten cavalry squadrons and a small artillery unit with a couple of cannon. In supreme command was Our Lady of the Seven Sorrows, the Virgin Mary, named early in the campaign as Generalissima of the Carlist armies, who, as before, marched under the slogan *Dios, Patria, Rey*. In effective command was the Infante Sebastian, son of the Princess de Beira, whom Don

Carlos hoped soon to bring out from England and marry. Sebastian, who had recently defeated General de Lacy Evans and a mixed British and Spanish force at Oriamendi near the town of San Sebastian, had as his chief of staff General Moreno, who had held high rank in the service of King Ferdinand. A notable absentee was Gomez. After returning with the rich spoils of his far-flung marches, and with more men and horses than he had set out with, this brilliant general was rewarded by being thrown into prison. Don Carlos had accused him of failing to secure the Asturias and Galicia for the Carlists, of appropriating much of his southern booty for his own aggrandisement, and for being too kind to prisoners. Again the finger of suspicion pointed at Cabrera who, diverted from his attempt to see Don Carlos personally, had, it was said, submitted unfavourable reports about the campaign in Andalucia, criticizing Gomez in particular for sparing the lives of prisoners captured there.

The Royal Expedition was remarkable in many ways; not only for its composition but for the route it took. The unlikely procession left Estella in the middle of May 1837. It did not make a direct line for Madrid, but made a leisurely progression south-eastwards through Navarre and Aragon, stopping at churches and cathedrals on the way for prayer and intercession. Inevitably there were clashes with Cristino forces, notably at Huesca, where the Cristino General Iribarren led a brave but foolish cavalry charge and was killed by a lance, with twenty-seven officers and some two hundred and fifty men of the British Legion among his thousand casualties; and at Barbastro, where General Oráa was defeated, but where French and German members of the foreign legions on either side slaughtered each other in such numbers that they ceased to exist as effective fighting forces. After a push into Catalonia had received another severe check, at Grá, the Expedition reached the Ebro towards the end of June, mauled but more or less intact, making camp on the eastern bank at a point opposite Cherta, some five or six miles above Tortosa.

The Expedition had suffered near disaster at an earlier river crossing – that of the Cinca, when the Carlist rearguard was almost exterminated and many men lost in the fast-flowing current as the Cristinos caught up with the Carlists. The wide waters of the Ebro offered a more serious threat, and Cabrera rose to the occasion magnificently and probably saved the whole Expedition from irretrievable disaster.

Bridges up and down the river were safely in Cristino hands, and it was left to Cabrera to get the unwieldy Expedition across this biggest natural obstacle of its route. He displayed true military genius in doing so. The Cristino military authorities had ordered all boats in Cherta and neighbouring places to be brought down river to Tortosa. Those that could not be moved were burned at their moorings, and it looked as if the Expedition might get trapped on the eastern bank by the pursuing armies. But Cabrera had foreseen this possibility; he had gone down to the port of San Carlos de la Rapita, south of Tortosa, and seized all the boats he could find there. Mules dragged them on wheels and carriages over the mountain roads up to the river near Cherta in this new Napoleonic manoeuvre.

Now, to ensure a safe crossing, Cabrera had to capture Cherta itself. Two Cristino divisions were driving towards the town, one coming down from Mora de Ebro led by his arch-enemy Nogueras, the other moving up from Tortosa under General Borso. Cabrera ordered one of his trusted aides, Pertegaz (he who had broken the news of his mother's death) to take up position on heights overlooking Nogueras' route and to defend them if necessary with his life. At the same time, Cabrera led his own force against Borso, and obliged him to retreat, as Pertegaz carried out his orders to the letter and prevented the two Cristino divisions from linking up. The skirmishing took place before the eyes of the Pretender, watching from a vantage point on the other side of the river. Urged on by his presence and by Cabrera's cries, the local Carlists captured Cherta, and the passage of the Ebro was assured. The boats from San Carlos de la Rapita were immediately brought into use, and Cabrera went across on the first, to kiss the hand of his king and offer him anew his loyalty and his service. Then the Pretender and his courtiers, generals and lesser officers, soldiers, guns, mules and horses were ferried over. Don Carlos received the Tortosan leader with an unaccustomed show of cordiality, and when the whole

Cabrera gets Don Carlos and the Royal Expedition – the unwieldy march on Madrid – across the Ebro.

Expedition was safely established in Cherta, rewarded him with the Grand Cross of the Order of San Fernando, naming him *comandante-general* of Aragon, Valencia and Murcia.

Great rejoicing followed. Bands played, there was dancing in the streets, and Don Carlos and his court went off to chant a *Te Deum* in the local church. The celebrations over, the Expedition renewed its winding march, its fighting strength considerably increased by the accession of Cabrera's men, who now formed the vanguard of Don Carlos' army.

Cabrera tried to impress on Don Carlos and his general staff the need to speed up progress, and he urged a night and day march on the capital; but the great city of Valencia proved a too-tempting target, so the ponderous Expedition made yet another diversion, convinced that it would fall. A taste of what was to come was given by the defenders of Castellon de la

Plana, the second biggest city on that part of the coast. They showed no disposition to welcome the Pretender, and put up such resistance that the Carlists called off the attack after wasting more valuable days.

Likewise, the citizens of Valencia gave no hint that they were impressed by the Pretender and his forces encamped at their gates. Far from capturing it, the Royal Expedition almost met disaster, for Oráa and Borso came out to dislodge the enemy. They overtook the Carlists in the fields of Chiva, inflicting heavy losses on them, Oráa himself exacting ample satisfaction for his reverse at Barbastro. Again, diversionary tactics by Cabrera, who drew off the Cristinos by sudden attacks on other places around, saved the day. This battle gives another example of the unreliability of the casualty claims made by both sides throughout the war. Oráa reported to Madrid that he had taken 1000 prisoners and that 200 Carlists had deserted against Cristino losses of 850 killed and wounded. In a later despatch he precisely doubled the Carlist figures.

The mauled royal columns turned back into the Maestrazgo to recoup in the Cabrera headquarters of Cantavieja. There a certain coolness developed between Cabrera and the Carlos court which made the impetuous general reluctant to continue, so much so that he had to be ordered to accompany the Expedition when, after exhausting the town's provisions, it turned at last towards Madrid. On the way, still full of obtuse optimism, Don Carlos on 1 August issued a decree setting up a governing junta for Aragon, Valencia and Murcia, and naming his diplomatic representatives to the courts of Vienna, St Petersburg and Turin. He was ready to enter Madrid.

Some military successes cheered him on. North of the capital another Carlist general, Zarategui, had been making an independent approach with about 4000 men. This drew off part of the Queen's forces, and at the same time Don Carlos' troops scored a substantial success when one of Oráa's field generals, Buerens, ventured to attack the Expedition in the mountains around Herrera as it marched towards New Castile, and lost nearly a hundred officers and about 1500 men killed, wounded or captured. Among the Carlist dead was one of Cabrera's deputies, General Quilez, who had always found it difficult to accept his chief's ruthless authority. Moving on, pursued by Oráa, and with Espartero moving down from the north, the Expedition crossed the Tagus at Fuentidueña, south-east of Madrid, on 10 September and two days later established camp within sight of the capital, four months after setting out from Navarre. Cabrera sent Forcadell and an advance guard of 3000 on to Vallecas, almost on the outskirts, and Zarategui joined the main body, bringing the strength of the Carlist armies outside Madrid to about 20,000 men. Then, having achieved the miracle of bringing his troops and their followers, their supplies and ammunition, his court and baggage, to the end of a march of some 800 miles, much of it through hostile country, Don Carlos allowed the miracle to dissolve in indecision and delay.

There is no doubt that had the Carlists immediately gone into the assault on Madrid, they would have taken it without much trouble. But, as before, Don Carlos waited for a sign from the people; and, as elsewhere, it did not come. Agents passed between his camp headquarters and the royal palace, with Don Carlos putting out feelers to Maria Cristina. Although the Queen Regent was fearful of the bloodshed which seemed inevitable, she gave no hint of compromise, and Don Carlos himself had no intention of moderating his claim. He now had to decide whether to risk his all.

Cabrera had put up a plan for attacking the different Cristino divisions around the capital while they were not in a proper state of readiness and still under separate commands. The Carlist council did not like it, and the opportunity was lost. Cabrera's cavalry, more by accident perhaps than good tactics, had won a clash with Cristino mounted troops and captured a Cristino colonel and other soldiers, ending up at the Atocha Gate. This could have been the moment to attack, but the Carlist command dithered, and, in a day or two, to the consternation of Cabrera and to the surprise of most observers both inside and outside the city, Don Carlos sanctioned an order to retreat.

George Borrow, that English linguistic and literary genius and colporteur extraordinary, was in Madrid at the time. In *The Bible in Spain* he records his own astonishment that the Carlists, 'with the city almost at their mercy, did not take it and put an end to the war at once'. Borrow may have been surprised, but he was not short of an explanation. 'The truth is,' he wrote, 'the Carlist generals did not wish the war to cease, for as long as the country is involved in bloodshed and anarchy they could plunder and exercise that lawless authority so dear to men of force and brutal passion.'

There may have been a grain of truth in Borrow's allegations, but certainly they were not true of Cabrera. The Tiger could not believe his ears when he heard the order to retreat; and angry and bitterly indignant, he set off with his troops to return to Aragon, leaving the generals and court officials around Don Carlos to pursue their intrigues and self-interest, and find their own way back to Navarre.

Espartero, having staged a triumphant march-past for the Queen Regent in Madrid, set off in pursuit. He almost caught Don Carlos at Brihuega, then chased him 350 miles back to the Ebro, which the Pretender crossed back into Navarre at the end of October 1837.

10
Correspondent on Horseback

In England, readers of the *Morning Post* (now the *Daily Telegraph*) were able to follow the Royal Expedition in some detail, for this famous London newspaper had appointed a correspondent to ride with the Carlist troops. His despatches, more often than not unsigned, and identified simply by the initials 'C.L.G.' when they were, filled column after column of the paper between July and November 1837. 'C.L.G.' was Charles Lewis Gruneisen, a young Englishman who joined the Expedition in its early stages, rode with it to the outskirts of Madrid, and then covered its retreat. With the soldiers he risked all the hazards of the march, went hungry at times, came under fire at others, and was often near capture.

The correspondent was standing near Cabrera when the order to retreat from Madrid was given. Furious and with his eyes flashing, the Carlist chief shouted 'What is the meaning of this?' and uttered a string of curses which defied the correspondent's interpretation. Gruneisen also had difficulty in comprehending the command's conduct, but he was in no doubt as to the fateful turning-point – the Carlist débâcle at Alcala de Henares, fifteen miles east of Madrid, when they had a favourable chance of attacking Espartero's advance troops as he moved down from the north. Only a short time earlier, Gruneisen had been quoting Carlist predictions that they would enter the city within three days. Now he was writing pessimistically: 'The unfortunate expedition to Alcala on September 19 [seven days after Cabrera had made his cavalry sortie], our failure to surprise it, has been attended with disastrous consequences. There was a want of decision and energy at a critical moment. Had the Chief of Staff attacked on the day that Cabrera's cavalry reached the very gates of Madrid, the Carlists would have entered the city with little difficulty and it is questionable whether Don Carlos having entered, Espartero's Army would have shown fight. The anxious desire of Don Carlos to prevent bloodshed in Madrid influenced General Moreno no doubt, but a golden opportunity was lost from a praiseworthy but mistaken humanity. At Alcala de Henares the death blow was given, I fear, to the entrance of Charles the Fifth in this campaign. This is my opinion, and as a faithful correspondent I consider myself bound to state it, although I am free to confess that I find few people at Royal Headquarters of the same mind.' Gruneisen's opinion was to be proved right; the Pretender would not enter Madrid in that campaign or any other. But few would agree with Gruneisen's suggestion that humanity was the prime reason for Don Carlos' failure, for the Carlists had shown no hesitation in causing bloodshed elsewhere.

Something of the hardships the retreating Carlist troops suffered came out in more than one of Gruneisen's despatches. He records a scene at a night stop at Renales on the road back to Navarre: 'The rain coming down in torrents, the men left their encampments and crowded into the filthy receptacles where the officers scarcely found shelter from the perilous storm. In a mean hovel, where even in Ireland pigs would not be deposited, I passed the night in a hayloft having for society two companies of soldiers. The Black Hole of Calcutta must have been a dreadful place indeed for I can institute a comparison having been in the hole at Renales.'

In a later report the correspondent gives a picture of himself scurrying his horse up a mountain track to escape falling shells and musket fire. Then this despatch about a shared experience with another young Englishman, Charles Frederick Henningsen, a captain of Lancers who before he was twenty had fought for a year with Zumalacárregui in the north and then written a book about it: 'My friend, Captain Henningsen, and myself had a narrow escape this day. We were desperately hungry and having found two as half-starved chickens as we were, made a fry of the whole with some potatoes. Every mouthful we consumed, the padrone rushed in exclaiming "Los enemigos! Los enemigos!" We retorted "The chickens!

The chickens!" and munched on till a volley of musketry was heard. There was no mistake in this; out we rushed, mounted and were off, scarcely knowing where to go . . .'

And then this gem, after another restless night's lodging: 'What is dreadful here is the quantity innumerable of those lively insects whose astonishing industry may be seen in Regent Street at the price of one shilling. With all due respect for our native talent, I deny that the tutored manoeuvres of the Regent Street tribe come up to the natural moves of the Spanish fleas. The war has rendered them perfect adepts in a "civil" contest. From the King to the paysan the cry is "They come". Everyone is infested and everybody is fully alive to the visitation. The other night I was attacked by two columns, one performing a flank movement and the other advancing in front. After essaying various means to induce the enemy to abandon their positions, I resolved upon an immediate engagement by divesting myself of my clothes. I gained a signal victory, they were completely dislodged and I took prisoners whom, by virtue of the Durango decree, being foreigners, I consigned to instant death.'

Though clearly a committed Carlist himself, this resourceful correspondent on horseback served the fortunate readers of the *Morning Post* very well. Not only did he give them reasonably fair and accurate accounts of a foreign war, he also entertained them right royally during his progress with the Royal Expedition. The memory of Cabrera outside the gates of Madrid was to stay fresh in the mind of the correspondent for all time, and forty years later he was still saying that he would never forget the fury in the Tortosan chief's eyes on the night of the retreat from the capital.

Don Carlos' withdrawal and Cabrera's return to Aragon to continue the struggle in his own way raises the twin question: was the Pretender alone responsible for Carlist indecision, not only here but throughout the campaign; and whence came Cabrera's decision, his resolute, continuing will to fight? The answer to the first half must be a qualified 'yes'. Except for his stubborn conviction, admittedly upheld by some legal and constitutional authorities, that he was the rightful king of Spain, Don Carlos presented a picture of an irresolute, fumbling man rarely able to make up his mind and bending to pressures of the moment, inhibited by his religion and given to long bouts of prayer seeking divine guidance which, apart from frequent expression of pious hopes, he never gave any sign of receiving. It may have been that he was completely in the hands of incompetent, timid and rival advisers, as was his English namesake Charles, the Young Pretender, when threatening London nearly a hundred years earlier, his chances ruined by disunion and jealousy among the adherents of the House of Stuart and by numerous military mistakes. Certainly, from the Infante Sebastian and General Moreno downwards, Don Carlos' military chiefs were of widely varying ability if not some incompetence. The Carlist officers generally were excellent in the field and men of indomitable bravery, but when it came to strategy they displayed no foresight whatsoever, a considerable factor in their many defeats.

Cabrera, himself no strategist, was nevertheless an exception when it came to sheer military skill and the will to fight – and to fight again and again. He was a short man, no more than five feet four inches tall, a bit bow-legged from his horsemanship, and with jet black hair and moustache. An eyewitness who watched him take the Royal Expedition across the Ebro gave this picture of him: At the head of a little group of horseman was a young man, mounted on a white horse. He had black hair, big brilliant eyes, and flashing white teeth, his beard a mere down. His small stature and delicately proportioned limbs gave an appearance so childlike that it would have been difficult to recognize in him the daring chief had it not been for the respect and enthusiasm shown by his followers. Cabrera wore a white *boina* with golden tassel, a short green jacket, scarlet trousers with silver braid, his shirt open at the neck to show a sinewy throat. He carried no arms on his person, but stuck in the prow of his saddle, which was covered by a wolfskin, were two large pistols, a sword and a sabre.

This observer averred that Cabrera's eyes were black, but according to a description issued some years later by the French police, who had the opportunity of studying him at closer quarters, they were grey-brown, and 'never looked his *interlocoteur* in the face'. That may have been so, but certainly he had no hesitation in looking straight at pressing military problems. As to the will which kept him going, perhaps he was one who, to quote the English statesman Bolingbroke writing about Spaniards a hundred years before Cabrera was born, '. . . knew not how to lose or when to yield'.

More probably, the will grew from his realization that there was no other option open to him but to fight on. He had no future except with the Carlist forces, for he was branded in the eyes of the Cristinos as an enemy, a barbarian, and this alone would have earned him nothing less than execution had he fallen into their hands. Therefore he could do nothing but go on fighting and there was likewise no point in his changing his brutal methods. As to what moved him in his youth and why Carlist, the key here must be his natural aggression, the desire to be against the established order, and his priestly training. This last was by no means least, for the convents were notorious as breeding grounds for Carlism, and the Tortosa seminary was no exception. When the fighting came, clerics went out with the chiefs and their guerrilla bands, often taking an active and bloody part in the fighting themselves, advising when they did not. The Bishop of Leon left his see to head the clerical team that always travelled with Don Carlos. He was with him at Madrid and went everywhere else with him, even into exile. Cabrera, the spoiled priest, had less use for them, and Cabrera the brigand suffered no such inhibitions as restrained Don Carlos from quick and ruthless action.

11

Count

Smarting from the débâcle of Madrid, Cabrera now took notice of orders from Navarre only when it suited him. He had formidable forces at his disposal at the beginning of 1838: about 13,000 infantrymen in sixteen battalions, 2000 horsemen forming nine or ten cavalry squadrons, and 400 artillerymen manning a dozen or so cannon, cast in the foundries of Cantavieja. He even formed some sort of navy, creating a coastal force out of sequestered fishing boats and other small craft; in command was his stepfather, Felipe Caldero, the boatman from Tortosa. This arm of Cabrera's combined forces soon paid for its keep by raiding a convoy of vessels headed by the mailship from Valencia as it was nearing the Ebro estuary, capturing cargoes of silk, flour and rice. But Felipe's navy failed to deliver the goods when, in the same area, it had to stand off and watch helplessly as coastguard vessels scared away a British gun-runner carrying 1000 muskets acquired for Cabrera in England.

With the Cristino divisions not properly redeployed after their pursuit of the Pretender, Cabrera's eyes inevitably turned towards Morella. This time, the fifth column succeeded in unlocking the gates. To the watching Carlist forces a gunner from the fortress presented himself one day. He had a plan, which he said he was prepared to guarantee with his life, for taking the castle and the town. The subaltern to whom he talked thought the idea impracticable, but Cabrera took up the man on his offer. The gunner was to lead the operation himself; he would be generously rewarded if it succeeded, otherwise his guarantee would be invoked. During the night of 25 January the gunner took a raiding party of twenty men to a spot at the foot of the castle walls and put up a ladder. Up he went followed by the others. The gunner crept up on the sole sentry at that spot dozing in his box and silently knifed him.

As he concealed the body, the others locked up the garrison in their dormitories; the castle was in the invaders' power. When the Cristino governor of the town, Colonel Portillo, brought up about 200 of his men, it was too late. The gates of the castle were barred against him, and he was greeted with a hail of hand grenades taken from the armoury and with cries of 'Long live the King, long live Cabrera!' The governor and his men beat a hasty retreat and moved out to the next Cristino town as the Carlists took over the whole of Morella.

Cabrera, again, was not present, busy at some other place – this time assaulting the coastal fortress of Benicarló which, although having a garrison of fewer than sixty men, put up a resistance which earned the expressed admiration of Cabrera, if no change in the way he dealt with them when they capitulated. This they did two days after the fall of Morella, which Cabrera then learned about for the first time.

On the last day of January, Cabrera made a triumphal entry into Morella, amid the clamour of its cheering people. This great success was followed by many others, until he had a string of Cristino forts, towns and villages in his hands, the reward of brilliant feats of arms that would have made the name of Cabrera ring truly around the world if they had not been tarnished by so much cruelty and un-necessary bloodshed.

With Morella as his capital, Cabrera set up what was in effect a state, appointing his own ministers – he had sacked the governing junta appointed by the Pretender on his way to Madrid – and naming his own prelates and clergy. His new headquarters was organized more completely and thoroughly than Cantavieja. Morella took on a form and colour which vied with the court of Don Carlos himself, whose authority Cabrera now rarely acknowledged. There was a big headquarters staff wearing rich and showy clothing and jewellery, and equipped with magnificent horses – altogether a picture of grandeur. Cabrera's troops were fitted out with splendid uniforms made in his own factories from cloth captured in raids on the cities and towns of Valencia. All had blue jackets and white trousers, but were identifiable as units by their headgear. Grenadiers had blue *boinas* with red tassels; fusiliers white tassels on blue; artillery all blue; while the cavalry wore red *boinas*. Cabrera himself wore a red or white one with golden tassel, according to his fancy, and almost always rode a white horse.

A few of his senior officers found all this, allied to his known predilection for the barbaric, a little difficult to stomach. One such was Cabañero, said to have once publicly challenged Cabrera about Carnicer's death, and then to have taken to the habit of changing his sleeping place at the last minute during night camps in the mountains lest an assassin's hand reach out for him in the darkness. Shortly after the capture of Morella, Cabañero decided to chance his arm in audacious operation which he hoped would draw off some of the glory from Cabrera. He decided to go for the great city of Zaragoza, the capital of Aragon. He got together a force of some 3000 infantrymen and 250 horsemen and made his approach in the middle of the night. An assault group got over the walls and opened a gate, and Cabañero sent his troops into the city. They got an unexpected reception from the surprised inhabitants. National guards, called from sleep by the cries of the sentries, scrambled to their windows in their nightshirts and poured a hail of lead down on to the invaders. At daybreak they came out on to the streets and drove them out. A local historian of the time relates this story of the confusion that prevailed during the night, with the drums of attackers and defenders sounding out alarms and orders: Two drummers came upon each other as they plied their sticks vigorously but to very different beats. 'Why do you beat Withdraw?' demanded one. 'Why do you beat To Arms?' asked the other. 'I obey my orders.' 'And I mine.' A passing lantern showed up the Carlist *boina* of the one and the National Guard uniform of the other, and they stared at each other until the light of recognition dawned. Then, instead of reaching for their swords, they continued their march side by side, each beating out his contradicting orders. Cabañero lost a third of his force in the attack, almost 300 dead and 700 prisoners, and incurred Cabrera's renewed displeasure.

Cristino generals had one by one broken themselves on Cabrera's anvil; now it was the turn of Oráa himself. Espartero, now overall commander of the Cristino forces in Spain, numbering in all close on 100,000, against a total

Carlist force of perhaps 30,000, was not prepared to leave the capture of Morella unchallenged, and he ordered General Oráa to retake it. This was not to be an isolated action but part of a concerted plan to take Cantavieja, Estella, the Carlist capital in Navarre, and Berga in Catalonia at the same time. Oráa, having circulated a proclamation to the inhabitants of Aragon and Valencia, another to his army, and a third to Cabrera's, moved towards Morella with over 17,000 men in all; infantrymen, cavalry, engineering units, and twenty-five pieces of artillery. They were in three divisions, with another in reserve; the first under Borso, the second Pardiñas, and the third San Miguel, with cavalry and artillery generals, and a brigadier in charge of the reserve. They approached from all sides and made a rendezvous on the heights surrounding the town on 27 July 1838. Cabrera's defending force numbered about 10,000, and he cleverly decided to employ the bulk of it outside in the hilly approaches to Morella, where he placed fourteen battalions, his cavalry squadrons, and thirty pieces of artillery of varying calibre. He left eighteen guns inside, with five battalions of town and fortress defenders.

Oráa began the attack in the last week of July, and was engaged by Cabrera's external forces. There followed a series of confused actions in which it was difficult to tell the besieged from the besiegers. There were stand-up battles between infantry units of the two sides, although any similarity between the operations of the fusiliers with their flint-lock muskets and those of the modern rifleman, with his rapid-firing weapons, is entirely accidental. The fusilier, after he had fired, had to reload by biting the end off a ball-and-paper cartridge, pouring some of the gunpowder into the flashpan and the rest down the muzzle of the gun, then ramming home the ball and paper. Although it was reckoned that a good man could do this in twenty or thirty seconds, if continuous fire were needed the fusiliers had to be drawn up in ranks several rows deep; when the front line fired they stepped to the rear to reload as the next took over, then gradually moved up until it was their turn again. This was the idea, and sometimes rapid though somewhat inaccurate fire was achieved; but more often than not there was chaos and, with no time to reload this short-range weapon, frantic men fell back to slashing about with the

Morella, fortress on top of an Aragon cliff.

bayonet as the enemy came up with them. Similarly inaccurate firing from unrifled artillery pieces, and cavalry charging about, added to the confusion.

Cabrera's demoniac energy, his knowledge of the difficult terrain, his men's stubborn defence, and the supply problems of the Cristinos made it an incredibly difficult task for Oráa. Nevertheless, after battering away for three weeks, his artillerymen and engineers managed to make a breach in the walls near one of the portals. It was not very promising, though a surprise attack might have forced it. But although Oráa chose dark of night for the attempt, he launched his assault with military bands playing. Three columns were sent in, only to be thrown back by a veritable volcano of fire, not from the guns but from a blazing inferno that the defenders had set going in the breach after piling up the remains of wooden buildings destroyed in the bombardments. The

Cristinos fell back, their three assault columns almost wiped out by gunfire from the walls. This was on 15 August; at daybreak on the 17th, his engineers having levelled off some baulking hillocks, Oráa again sent in his assault troops. They were greeted with a hail of musketry fire – with hand grenades and other missiles tossed down from the parapets, and the Cristino general was forced to the conclusion that he could not take Morella with the equipment at his command. He gave the order to raise the siege and before the month was out all his troops and his mule-drawn besieging train were back at their starting points.

Cabrera, leading his external forces, watched them go, and then made a solemn entry into Morella. He was greeted by the population on their knees in obeisance, and the clergy conducted him in triumph to the cathedral, where a *Te Deum* was sung. Praise was heaped on him and messages of congratulation flowed from Don Carlos, his ministers and his generals in Navarre. There was an order from Don Carlos which he chose not to ignore and which re-established their rapport. It promoted him to lieutenant-general and commanded that henceforth he be known as Count of Morella.

This defeat compelled the Cristinos to call off their operations at Cantavieja, Estella and Berga too, although these had never really got going because of the delay at Morella. For Oráa it proved disastrous. There was criticism of him by the government and in the press, in fact a countrywide outcry which resulted in his losing his command. There was nothing new in this process – the politicians in Madrid almost invariably demanded the scalp of generals who reported a lack of success. But although he had carried out the operation with considerable courage, there may have been some justice in this dismissal; there were three English commissioners with the Cristino army of the centre at the time – Colonel Lacy, Colonel Alderson (the teller of the story about Cabrera and his host's daughter) and Lieutenant Askwith – and they all criticized Oráa. They said he had showed a great want of foresight and that the assault on 15 August was 'insane' because the breach in the walls was utterly impracticable; and in the second attack even the scaling ladders were too short. Oráa had probably acted precipitately because he was conscious of growing and alarming scarcities of ammunition and provisions.

At the time the Cristinos were converging on Morella the wheat had been cut and was lying in the fields. The attackers did not think of harvesting it, and Oráa himself did nothing about it; his troops let the corn lie and used it to bed down their horses and mules as well as feed them, burning what was left. When they had run short of food, they came back to search for grains in the trampled, blackened fields. Provisions had not been the only problem for Oráa; to get just one of his big guns up some of the steeper hills needed a team of at least twenty mules, and hundreds more were needed to transport the ammunition. But he got them all in position and fired over 2000 shells against the fortress before admitting defeat. Prominent in the attack, at his own request, had been the former governor of Morella, Colonel Portillo, and his men, anxious to restore reputations tarnished when the fortress was captured; Portillo lost his life in the second assault after miraculously surviving the first wild rush into the burning breach.

Espartero put in as Oráa's successor General Van Halen, a man with almost as cruel a record as Cabrera himself. If the Cristinos expected Cabrera to relax after the capture of Morella, they did not know their man. Within days of Oráa's withdrawal, he was again at the gates of the city of Valencia, his troops surprising women bathing in a stream, sending them running naked and screaming for their honour, if not for their lives. Valencia shut its gates and not a soul moved in or out of the city for three days. In that time, the Carlists plundered the rich land for miles around and were making their way back to the Maestrazgo with cattle, horses, crops and money, passing audaciously between Cristino columns moving back to base after the unsuccessful assault on Morella.

Soon Cabrera was able to bring to battle one of the divisional leaders at Morella, Pardiñas, a young Cristino general with a very high reputation for ability and courage. Cabrera, jealous of this reputation, sought him out near Maella; their troops, about equal in numbers, fought for six hours and 1000 dead were left on the field of battle. Among these was Pardiñas who, wounded and with his horse shot from under him, had propped himself against a tree and was defending himself with his sword when a lance was driven through him. It was said that Cabrera tried to save him; if that be so, would Pardiñas have suffered the same fate as the 150 officers and sergeants among the 3000 prisoners claimed to have been taken? For in another shocking display of cruelty Cabrera's men stripped them of their clothing and chased and killed them with musket, bayonet and lance. Pardiñas, however, was not lost to Cabrera's memory; he named one of his white horses after him.

Van Halen, in his turn, wreaked bloody vengeance on the hapless Carlist prisoners who fell into his hands, and the combat deteriorated into sheer bestiality; so much so that efforts were intensified to humanize the war in the east as it had been, long since, in the north. There, as far back as April 1835, the Carlist and Cristino commanders in chief, Zumalacárregui and Valdes, had signed Lord Eliot's convention to stop the shooting of prisoners and arrange for their exchange. During the Peninsular War, the British government was shocked at what its own troops had been doing in Spain, and the move to humanize the new war was started by their commander in chief, Wellington, now Foreign Secretary. Lord Eliot went out to Spain with the Duke's written instructions. Before he was through Sir Robert Peel's government had fallen and Palmerston was back at the Foreign Office, but he instructed Eliot to carry on his efforts.

Now, as the year 1838 came to a close, Villiers, ambassador in Madrid, was trying to get the convention extended to the eastern provinces. It was slow going; it took the senior English commissioner with the army of the centre, Colonel Lacy, three months to persuade Van Halen and Cabrera, each blaming the other, to give up the practice of massacring prisoners. Lacy, a Royal Artillery officer, first of all secured the release of a captured Carlist officer, and used him to convey a message to Cabrera, saying that if he would cancel his order not to give quarter, Van Halen would instantly and gladly adopt the rules of civilized warfare. Cabrera received the officer at Morella on 31 December; but he resented the method of communication and sent him back, annotating his papers with this message:

'He presented himself, and this mode of treating in respect to the
subject he has explained not being proper and decorous, he will
return to the point from which he came.'

– El Conde de Morella.

Lacy took the hint and wrote a personal letter to Cabrera,
using some terms of praise for the Carlist general and, in his
final communication, perhaps bearing in mind his priestly
training, appealing to his Christianity. Whether it was this, or
the slightly flattering remarks, that touched Cabrera is not
evident; but ultimately he agreed and the convention was
signed, first by Van Halen and then by Cabrera, although the
latter scrawled on it 'Excepted: Nogueras and myself.'

As a generalization, it can be said to have worked. There
were violations from time to time, and it probably resulted in
fewer prisoners being taken on the field of battle. But in
detention the Cristino prisoners seemed to suffer worse than
before; they were frequently ill-treated and kept short of food.
When exchanged, they presented a sorry sight compared with
Carlist prisoners who had been treated according to the spirit
as well as the letter of the convention. It did not stop Cabrera
from seeking out Cristinos and destroying them in combat.
Only thirty-two years of age, he was now a general, a count,
and a Knight Grand Cross of the Order of San Fernando; and
although the great dream he had doubtless had outside the
gates of Madrid – 'Don Carlos on the throne and I the great
general at his shoulder' – had faded badly, he still had high
hopes. He at least was winning battles.

But things began to go wrong. Don Carlos' army, which had
stood so expectantly outside Madrid, was, by defections and
casualties, more than halved in strength from the 14,000 men
who had set out from Navarre almost six months earlier. As
the court re-established itself in Estella, the failure of the
Expedition took its inevitable toll, and quarrelling erupted
among the generals and courtiers as scapegoats were sought
and named. There was a purge of senior officers; the Infante
Sebastian lost his command and General Moreno was

dismissed. Other officers – the luckier ones – found themselves in prison; the unlucky were shot.

Out of this maelstrom emerged a new commander in chief, General Rafael Maroto, veteran of the campaigns in the Spanish American colonies and of the War of Independence. For Don Carlos it was a disastrous choice. Maroto set out to show that he was truly in command. He began reorganizing the Carlist forces, bloodily exterminated half a dozen other generals and senior officers who were getting in his way, and brought back some who had long since fallen foul of the Carlist court. Don Carlos at first denounced him as an assassin and traitor, but almost immediately had no option but to withdraw these charges and confirm him in office. Whereupon Maroto forced Don Carlos to dismiss some of his extremist advisers and replace them with more moderate thinkers.

Presently Maroto deemed that the reorganized Carlist troops were ready for action, and set off into the heart of the Basque country, ostensibly to confront the Cristino armies of the north under Espartero, with whom he had served in Peru. There were some minor engagements, for success in which Maria Cristina named Espartero Duke of Victory; but the big battle never took place. Feelings were changing in the hitherto Carlist strongholds of the north; and whether Maroto sensed this and acted on it, or whether he had been planning such a move from the start, he alone could tell. Certainly, the Carlist troops in the north were now displaying little heart, and Maroto could not inspire them as Cabrera continued to do in the east. So, humanitarian or betrayer of the cause according to the point of view, Maroto made overtures to the Queen's general which led to an agreement to end the war in the north.

Don Carlos got wind of the negotiations, and, putting on his uniform and all the trappings of royalty, confronted Maroto's troops in the field. He asked them to renew their allegiance, and declare themselves ready to fight on for 'God, Country, and King'. He was greeted with a sultry silence; red-faced with embarrassment, he asked one of Maroto's staff officers what it meant. Reaching around for an answer, the officer replied sheepishly: 'Sire, they don't understand Castilian!' 'Then ask them in Basque,' commanded Don Carlos. The officer did so, but put the question in a different form. 'Do you want peace, men?' he asked; and the troops responded with a thunderous *'Bay, Jauna!'* A defeated and dejected Don Carlos rode off with his escort back to Estella.

A few days later the agreement was signed and on 31 August 1839 it was consummated at Vergara. The Cristino and Carlist troops and cavalry marched into position to face each other as military bands played, the colours of the various uniforms – particularly the reds, whites and blues of the Carlist *boinas* – illuminating the ceremony.

The two generals moved forward on their horses to meet, and Espartero put his arms round Maroto's shoulders and embraced him. As he did so, he invited the Carlist troops to do likewise: 'Go and embrace your brothers as I do your general,' he commanded. Carlists and Cristinos broke ranks with enthusiasm, and ran to embrace each other.

This was the historic Embrace of Vergara; it was to be the beginning of the end of the first Carlist war. Under it, some 1000 Carlist officers had their ranks and titles confirmed, and officers and men had their pay made up and were offered service in Espartero's army; while the Basque people had their *fueros,* their regional privileges, guaranteed. Among the Carlist officers who chose service with the Queen was Cabañero, captor of Cantavieja and defender of Morella, driven there in disgust by Cabrera's atrocities. An observer marked his tall, gaunt figure astride his horse, his countenance heavy, perhaps casting the shadow of Cabrera's grim revenge to come.

Less than a year before, Don Carlos had married the Portuguese Princess de Beira, sister of his dead wife, and like her also his niece. Only his devotion to the cause of Rome, it was said, secured the necessary papal dispensation. Now, with her, his three sons and her son, the Infante Sebastian, the remnants of his court, and a few thousand Navarrese troops, with Villareal and Elio among the senior officers, Don Carlos entered France. They crossed at a place called Dancharinea, where only a small stream divided the two countries, just two hours ahead of Espartero's pursuing troops. Scattered belongings and piles of weapons gave evidence of their frantic passage.

Don Carlos, bitter and dejected, could see Maroto as none

other than a Judas, his humiliation reflected in his denunciation of his erstwhile commander-in-chief: 'The infamous traitor who had sold for foreign gold and recognition of military rank, God, the king, the country and the *fueros*'.

Certainly bribery came into it, in the sense that Maroto and his men were guaranteed their ranks and pay, including considerable sums outstanding from their service with Don Carlos. But there is little in the circumstances to support the suggestion of a gigantic scheme of corruption that in all cost Maria Cristina thirty million *reals*. Espartero probably had no more than eight million *reals* at his disposal for the pay and back-pay of the Carlist troops and for 'inducements' to their officers, and it is clear that Maroto, had he remained loyal to Don Carlos, would have had considerable difficulty in getting them to fight on in the changing attitude of the north towards Carlism.

12

Illness...Defeat

Cabrera, too, denounced Maroto and his followers as traitors, and vowed to shoot any of them who fell into his hands. He rejected the agreement and refused to give in, doing all he could to stop the circulation among the peasantry of the true story of the collapse in the north, or, where he was powerless to do so, to counteract its effect. His military activity, always intense, was never more apparent than in the three months immediately after Vergara. He moved about with lightning rapidity, and led the Cristino generals along so many false trails that at times they were chasing their own tails like packs of hounds which had lost the scent. In some areas he so fired the minds of the people that he, rather than Don Carlos, became the emblem and the cause; and more than one fortress had the slogan *Muera Don Carlos, Viva Cabrera* daubed on its walls. On the Cristino side, however, he became so hated that schemes were mooted in Madrid, and monies collected, for his assassination. One or two unfortunate strangers who arrived in Morella were summarily tried and executed on suspicion of being hired assassins.

Meanwhile, the command of the Cristino army of the centre had again changed hands. Van Halen, soon after signing the agreement on prisoners with Cabrera, had called off a projected assault on the Carlist stronghold of Segura, fifty miles west of Morella, and although all his junior officers and the English commissioner attached to his army had submitted written reports to him that the assault was impracticable, the Madrid politicians decreed that he must go. First of all he was replaced by none other than Nogueras, an indiscretion by Madrid which scared many people into thinking that because of his hatred for him Cabrera would tear up the agreement and return to a war of no quarter. But illness removed Nogueras within a couple of months, and the command was given to the young General Leopoldo O'Donnell, already beginning to make his considerable imprint on war and politics. He was already a victor over Cabrera in that he had beaten off the Carlist general's biggest attack on Lucena, a fortified town he had coveted almost as strongly as Morella, but which had never yielded in more than a dozen assaults. As a result O'Donnell was now Count of Lucena.

Espartero and his divisions, released by the Embrace of Vergara, were soon moving down to join O'Donnell in battle against the Carlists of Aragon. Cabrera, now in control of the main fortresses of the Maestrazgo and a string of lesser ones for miles around, made his plans to meet them. Anticipating Espartero's main objectives, he armed and provisioned Morella and Cantavieja to the full, prepared, as he told his men, to defeat Espartero or die in the attempt. He did almost die, but without going into battle.

Whatever it was that had made Cabrera tick, and tick so furiously, over the past years suddenly stopped working, and he was struck down with an indefinable illness. The first symptoms appeared in mid-December during a tour of inspection north of Morella. He complained of severe headaches, and was seen to be affected by cold shivers. His doctors ordered him to return to Morella. He reached the village of Herves and could go no farther. He was put to bed with a high fever, and on Christmas Eve he received the last rites of the Catholic Church. The symptoms were preciously like those of typhus, but his doctors could not agree on a diagnosis, let alone a treatment. Maybe it was that years of ferocious activity and dissolute living had caught up with him; that the pressure of recent events and coming battles had borne him down; or that he was devoured by the breakdown that most rebels suffer sooner or later. Vergara, if not the direct cause, was probably the catalyst.

Cabrera's doctors tried various remedies, including bloodletting by the application of leeches. There was some alleviation of his condition after Christmas, and, fearing an enemy attempt to capture him, it was decided to press on to Morella. He was taken over snow-covered mountain roads and reached the great fortress town in the second week of January 1840. He entered Morella this time not as a conquering hero but as a broken man carried on a stretcher. His condition deteriorated, and in bouts of delirium he was heard to scream out military orders and counter-orders. His sisters nursed him, and services were held in public as well as in church to pray for his delivery.

It was around this time that Don Carlos' commander in Catalonia, the Conde de España, an aged and half-mad perpetrator of bloody crimes himself, among them the destruction of the town of Ripoll and the erection in its place of a single stone inscribed 'There stood Ripoll', was treacherously strangled, in another example of Carlist internecine strife, and his body thrown into the River Segre. Don Carlos himself, from his exile at Bourges in France, forged some of the links in the chain of events leading to the count's extinction; and he now named Cabrera commander-in-chief of Catalonia as well as Aragon, Valencia and Murcia. Cabrera's entourage, for obvious reasons, had not been spreading the news of their leader's illness, and it appears that Don Carlos was ignorant of it at Bourges. For his message naming Cabrera commander-in-chief reached the Count of Morella on his sickbed in the town of his title. It did, however, happen to coincide with an improvement in his condition. He was moved from the chill climate of the Maestrazgo mountains to the warmer air of San Mateo, down near the Mediterranean coast; then, significantly, when the Cristino forces were gathering, to the Ebro at Mora, twenty-five miles above Tortosa.

His absence from the Maestrazgo, where he had left Forcadell in charge, disconcerted his partisans there and in all other fortified places. The successful war reports stopped coming out of Morella, and information on how things were going had to be gleaned from Cristino despatches printed in the Government press. Espartero and O'Donnell were now in full cry. Their first big prize was Segura, for which Van Halen had been sacrificed, taken at the end of February. Then Castellote fell. Not easily though, for Espartero recorded stubborn resistance and the fact that nearly 3500 projectiles from his artillery were needed to subdue it. One by one Cabrera's other strongholds fell. Then Mora de Ebro was surrounded and entered. But Cabrera was no longer there. It had been put about that he had died; but a day or two earlier he had been taken out of town in a *tartana*, the Spanish two-wheeled covered cart, to La Cenia, where he was greeted as if risen from the dead. He now learned for the first time of the full extent of his military losses. Although he had again received extreme unction in Mora, he seems to have been well enough after leaving La Cenia to put on his grand uniform, get on his horse Pardiñas, and harangue the local troops at one stopping place, Chert. Man or monster has been the constant theme of enquiry into Cabrera's life story; there now followed one single incident which must condemn him.

Early in the month of the Vergara agreement the previous year, but well before it had been concluded, Cabañero's son Mariano had joined the Carlists in the Maestrazgo. After Vergara, Cabrera ordered his detention on suspicion that he might be a Cristino agent, sent to try to secure similar defections to those his father and other Carlist chiefs had made in the north. Now he encountered Mariano Cabañero in La Cenia. The sick general included him in his escort for the continued journey to Morella, and after haranguing the troops at Chert had the young man shot. Here we have a man who believed he was dying, and who had twice asked for, and been given, the last rites of the Catholic Church; here was a man now in a state of grace who could not find it in his heart to show mercy or offer the benefit of the doubt to the son of a former comrade who had seen him through the thick of the fighting in the early days of the Maestrazgo campaign.

A few days later, Cabrera was in Morella, to the accompaniment of peals of bells, artillery salutes, cheers and church services, and repeated displays of awed wonderment by the common people at his apparent resurrection. Their joy, however, was short-lived, for soon he had said goodbye for ever to the place of his great triumph and grandeur; but not before trying to instil some sort of confidence in its defenders by assuring them that help from thousands of Russian and French troops was on the way.

'*Voluntarios!*' he addressed them. 'Order and subordination! You will soon see me at the head of the army. Have confidence in your general as I also have in the chiefs I have placed in this fortification. If we have encountered some loss, it will be speedily recovered, and very soon there will not remain any enemies to be conquered.' He then toured the fortifications and departed. The garrison never saw him again.

Soon his beloved stronghold from early days, Cantavieja, was in Cristino hands, abandoned without a fight; and almost in the same breath Benicarló, San Mateo and a dozen other places, many by force, the rest abandoned as his troops deserted, first the raw recruits and then the seasoned fighting men. He moved back to La Cenia, where he lost a clash with O'Donnell and where, from another of the somersaults of Vergara, O'Donnell had a brother badly wounded fighting now for the Cristinos (another brother was the O'Donnell decapitated by the anti-Carlist mob in Barcelona). Then on again towards the Ebro, as Espartero brought up his forces to besiege Morella. Espartero was not going to risk his reputation at Morella by repeating any of Oráa's mistakes; he brought to bear on the fortress all the power he had at his immediate disposal. In the middle of May he moved in four divisions from the four points of the compass, about 20,000 men in all, and made sure of the constancy of his supplies by using another six or seven thousand to protect road communications. He brought up more than fifty pieces of artillery, including eight 24-pounder guns and some heavy howitzers, hiring thousands of mules and farm carts from the peasantry to drag them into position and transport the ammunition.

After Oráa's attack Cabrera had built a strong advance fortification on a commanding height some 2000 yards north of Morella – the redoubt of San Pedro. Espartero's first task was to reduce this. Its garrison of 270 men put up a brave show, but Espartero's big guns soon pounded them into unconditional surrender. Espartero then turned on Morella proper, concentrating on the fortress castle jutting into the sky from its rocky outcrop high above the houses, churches and convents of the town. When Oráa's assault troops had twice gone into the breach nearly two years earlier, they had been at the mercy of the guns from the castle above. Espartero now silenced them, one of the shots hitting a powder magazine and setting off an explosion. After several days of bombardment, with surprisingly little return fire from the garrison, one of the Carlist officers came down over a wall of the town and escaped to the Cristino lines. He brought a tale that the garrison was planning to escape that night under the cover of darkness in a bid to join Cabrera in the field. Espartero moved in his infantry closer to the walls and waited. Presently, one of the gates was slowly opened and the drawbridge let down. Over it came several hundred of the garrison troops, and dim in the background could be seen the outline of a huge mass of civilians, donkeys and mules laden with baggage, waiting to follow.

Espartero's fusiliers and gunners opened up, and the leading troops turned back in panic and confusion on those seeking to follow, and members of the garrison left inside fired on their own men, thinking they were facing a Cristino assault. The gate was forcibly closed, leaving the drawbridge choked to capacity. A chance shell fell on it, hurling soldiers, women, children and animals into the moat, many who had not been killed by the explosion being crushed or suffocated by the mass of bleeding bodies as survivors tried to claw their way out in blind terror.

As day broke on 30 May, there was a parley by the remaining defenders about terms of surrender, but Espartero sent in a peremptory demand that they deliver themselves forthwith. Over 2500 men and more than 100 officers of Cabrera's army marched out and laid down their arms, on the sole guarantee that their lives would be spared; they were followed out by several hundred civilians, among them women with babies in their arms or leading children by the hand. General Espartero, already Count of Luchana for a victory in the north in 1836, and Duke of Victory for later successes there, was immediately named Duke of Morella by Queen Cristina – one up on Cabrera's countship.

With the Duke of Morella and his army in hot pursuit, the Count of Morella and his generals, none of whom had stayed in the fortress, withdrew across the Ebro into Catalonia with about 5000 infantrymen and six or seven hundred cavalry, dropping into the river a number of National Guard prisoners as they went. The crossing-point was Cherta, where Cabrera had earned supreme recognition at Don Carlos' passage three long years before, skirting Tortosa, tomb of his mother and of his boyhood, on the way. He made for the old Carlist Catalan stronghold of Berga, where, before looking to the defences and

94

the placing of his troops, he found time to dismiss the junta that had sent the Conde de España to his death and throw most of its members into prison.

Berga, some fifty miles north of Barcelona, and with the French frontier only twenty miles farther on, was well provisioned and strongly armed when Cabrera got there. With his own troops, he could have raised about 16,000 to man its chain of more than twenty closely linked forts. Had he wished to choose his ground, this was the place, a far tougher proposition for the Cristinos than Morella could ever have been. As Espartero's army approached, it seemed that Cabrera was going to stand and fight. When the advance guard opened fire on one of the principal forts, observers on the Cristino side watching through telescopes saw him ride into view mounted on a handsome white horse. He was dressed in a blue frock coat, thrown back to display a white waistcoat; on his head was a white *boina*. Around him his staff officers and a cavalry escort clustered. The group appeared on a plateau near the fort as the men inside cheered. Cabrera dismounted, and, accompanied by an aide, moved down a slope to get a better view of the attackers. At this moment Espartero opened up with his mountain howitzers. A couple of shells fell near Cabrera, who instantly remounted and galloped off at full speed, followed with equal precipitation by his staff and escort. They vanished over the ridge, and did not reappear.

'They vanished for ever – and rested not until they had the Pyrenees at their back. The redoubtable Cabrera took to flight in the presence of a portion of the Queen of Spain's Army the instant that two grenades fell at some little distance from him . . . This I saw with my own eyes,' wrote one of the observers, the much-travelled John Moore, who wrote under the pseudonym *Poco Mas* – 'Little More', perhaps to distinguish himself from his illustrious namesake Sir John, buried at dead of night at Corunna not so many years before.

Espartero made his entry into Berga on 4 July 1840. He remained there a week, clearing up, and organizing its rehabilitation as a city of the Queen. Then the all-conquering general left to join Maria Cristina and the young Queen Isabel, who had just arrived in Barcelona after skirting the battle areas in their journey from Madrid.

In the small hours of 6 July Cabrera entered France at Palau, accompanied by his deputy Forcadell and a dozen or so other generals and chiefs. Cabrera's farewell address to his troops was too much for the emotions of some of them, and a few committed suicide in dramatic fashion. The rest, some 4700 foot soldiers and 300 cavalrymen, followed him across the frontier to hand over their arms to the French military authorities. Don Carlos' attempt to gain the throne of Spain was at an end.

Other Carlist groups straggled over the frontier during the next few days and weeks. Some chiefs held out for a time. Those who were not clever enough to fade into the hills, as Cabrera had been so adept in doing, were hunted down, summarily tried and executed. One chief, by name Liguina, who had long eluded pursuit in the mountains, had his fate delayed. 'As he is mad at the moment,' the Madrid account of his capture and conviction said, 'his execution is postponed until the return of reason!' The history books fail to record whether Liguina was sensible enough to retain his insanity, and so preserve himself from the firing squad or the newer method of executing traitors and criminals.

Hanging had been the traditional method of execution in Spain until Ferdinand's reign; but the liberal Cortes regarded it as inhuman, and introduced capital offenders to Madame Guillotine's vulgar, though no less expeditious, half-brother, Don Garrote.

The garrote was usually set up in a public square. It was a simple apparatus, consisting of a stout wooden stake rising high from the platform, with a stool at its base. At neck height, an iron collar with a turnscrew was fastened to the upright. The condemned man sat on the stool and his neck was locked into the collar's iron clutch. A quick half turn of the screw, and the victim was instantly transported to eternity.

Alexander Somerville, in his *History of the British Legion and War in Spain,* described the garroting of two men found guilty of treason during the epidemics that decimated the ranks of the legion at Vitoria in the bitter winter of 1835/6. The victims were the head baker to the Cristino army at Vitoria, José Elgoez, and his assistant. The baker, as well as providing bread for the British troops was, it seems, the contact man in

Don Garrote, Madame Guillotine's vulgar half-brother.

the town for arranging desertions to the Carlists, who were
offering deserters various sums of money according to their
rank. British officers set a trap for him, and he was caught in
the act of conducting a planted party of 'deserters' out of the
town. The bread, insufficiently kneaded and not properly
baked, had been blamed for many of the deaths among the
British troops, and Elgoez was rumoured to be poisoning it.
Poisonous substances were said to have been found at his
bakery when he was arrested, but Don José and his assistant
probably needed no such aid to worsen their doughy, half-
baked product, and they were tried and convicted solely on the
charge of being Carlist agents. They were garroted after first
being stripped naked in the marketplace and beaten with rods.

'The garrote,' wrote Somerville, 'is peculiar to Spain and its operation is certainly the most expeditious and unseemly way of putting criminals to death except by shooting now in use. On the morning of 28 March, two companies of troops and the 1st Lancers marched into the town of Vitoria and formed up round the platform. Muffled drums beat a dead march and after a wait of about five hours the two criminals attended by about twenty priests were seen moving slowly down an opening in the military ranks.'

The baker, a rich man unsuccessful in his attempts to purchase his life, apparently had bought his salvation. For Somerville recorded that in many churches the service for the dead was performed all day, while around the scaffolding the attending clergy prayed with great perseverance and apparent earnestness. Don José ascended first, and, after speaking with his confessor for about two minutes and taking the sacrament, his hands were bound down, the collar was put around his neck, the executioner twisted the handle of the screw, and the ill-fated baker was dead.

Immediately afterwards, his assistant was brought in, and the same operation was performed on him, the Spanish soldiers shouting loudly as the screw got the extinguishing turn. 'A cloth had been thrown over their faces previous to the execution,' said Somerville. 'It was now removed and the faces were seen without any distortion or even discolour of the skin, which proved that death must have been instantaneous. The bodies were left on the scaffold for three hours and a spectator who did not know the nature of the death would have supposed them to have been two men sitting comfortably down to be shaved . . .'

13

Exile

General Espartero, who very shortly after evicting Cabrera from Spain was also to push Maria Cristina into exile and take over the regency himself, had a lot in common with the Carlist leader. Both were small physically, with dark, olive-skinned faces. Both were of humble parents. And both were intended for the Church.

Baldomero Espartero was born on 27 October 1793 in the little town of Granatula in La Mancha, the province which Cervantes selected for the achievements of his hero Don Quixote. Baldomero's father has been variously described as carter, ploughman and wheelwright; he was probably all three. He was the last of a flock of children, and his father, too poor to pay for his youngest's education, sent him to his eldest, Manuel, who was a monk in Ciudad Real, the provincial capital, to arrange a course of study so that he might take holy orders. But the War of Independence had inflamed the young Espartero with patriotism, and at sixteen he left the seminary and went into a military school. Emerging as a sub-lieutenant, he enlisted in the 'Sacred Battalion', so called because it was composed entirely of young men who had been intended for the Church.

Espartero's military debut, like Cabrera's was not auspicious, but it did decide him on his path. For he stayed on in the army after Napoleon's troops had been evicted, and went across the Atlantic to join the campaign to crush the insurrection in the American colonies.

He soon became a colonel, and when he returned to Spain at the age of thirty-two he was a brigadier, bringing with him a considerable fortune, much of it from successful gambling at cards, which enabled him to make an advantageous marriage. With other officers of the campaign, he suffered the epithet *Ayacucho,* pinned on all who had subscribed to the 1824

Count of Morella, Cabrera. The Pretender awarded him the title for capturing the fortress.

capitulation at that place in Peru which led to Spain losing her American possessions for ever. Back home, the *Ayacuchos* brushed off the contemptuous epithet and banded together in a kind of colonial brotherhood, whose members managed still

Duke of Morella, Espartero. The Queen Regent made her general a duke for recapturing it.

to occupy most of the prime military positions around the throne before and after the death of Ferdinand VII.

Espartero himself quickly became a general, at much the same age as Cabrera, and the sheer force of character of both individuals was the decisive factor in many battles; although Thomas Raikes, in a condescending reference in his journal, said Espartero 'is very dilatory in action and sometimes passes whole days in bed drinking chocolate'. Espartero and Cabrera each took their prime titles from actions at Morella, both showing what good generals they were by being on the spot when great triumphs were won and somewhere else in the moment of catastrophic defeat. Proving their generalship right up to the end, each managed to die in his bed at a ripe old age. Here again, Espartero was victor: he did not fade away until his eighty-sixth year, against Cabrera's seventy-first.

When Cabrera was driven into France, he was rumoured to have brought big sums of money with him out of Spain. There is no firm evidence to support this. Nevertheless, General Balmaseda, Garcia's colleague in the raid on La Granja, had no doubts. Balmaseda had entered France shortly before Cabrera, his men miserable and hungry after being relentlessly pursued right up to the frontier. A French newspaper reported that he had little more than what he stood up in when he reached France. Balmaseda, reported the paper's correspondent on the spot, had nothing about his dress which bespoke the high command he had fulfilled. An old blue cloak and a red *boina* with black braid were his entire military costume. He had no embroidery on his collar, nor on his coat tails. All his stock appeared to consist in a few clothes, and his purse in the produce of the sale of the four magnificent horses with which he arrived in France. Somebody observed that it was extraordinary that he had nothing, while Cabrera appeared to have amassed immense sums. 'It is true,' Balmaseda replied. 'Cabrera will leave Spain with millions. I only bring away vermin!'

This self-portrait of a defeated general with nothing but fleas for troops was, however, not borne out by the reporter; he painted an image of more substantial presence: 'This Spanish general came through Tardets accompanied by two young Spanish ladies, both very beautiful, said to be his nieces. He is a tall man, with a downcast and sturdy look. He walked with his hands behind his back, looking upon the concourse of the people with a haughty air. It was seen that he was crossed by finding himself the object of such an eager curiosity and, biting his lips with passion, some insulting expressions towards the French were uttered by him.'

Balmaseda, who had wanted to seize Queen Isabel and her mother the Queen Regent from La Granja in the summer of 1836, had lain in wait for them with another kidnapping plan during their recent journey from Madrid to Barcelona as the Carlists were being driven out of Spain.

It had come very near to success, he said. Only the treachery of his fellow conspirator, another Carlist chief had defeated it. 'Every measure had been adopted,' said Balmaseda, 'and no other circumstance than this treachery could have saved Cristina and Isabel from falling into my hands.'

Asked what he would have done with the two queens, he replied: 'I should have written immediately to Espartero. I should have signified certain conditions. If he had not accepted them, or if this Army had made a single movement against me, I should have had them shot within twenty-four hours.' So spoke this Carlist chief who a moment before had declared that plunder and violence were not his business. Balmaseda had nothing but abuse and ridicule for Queen Cristina, and he predicted that within six months 'Spain will have shaken off the yoke of that woman and a republic will be proclaimed'. Although more than thirty years were to pass before his second prediction came true – the two-year republic of 1873 to 1875 before the monarchy was restored and Alfonso, then a youth at Sandhurst, became king – Balmaseda was very near the mark on his first. Well within his limit, Cristina had abdicated and sought sanctuary in France after a series of disagreements with Espartero, now ready for political power after his military victories over the Carlists. Yet within another three years Espartero himself was also to be forced into exile. He chose England, where, as Cabrera was to be, he was acclaimed by socialites and treated as something of a hero. Balmaseda went to Russia and obtained service with the Tsar, dying in St Petersburg within a very few years at the age of forty-six.

The paths of both Balmaseda and Cabrera had crossed that of George Borrow during his journeyings through Spain. Borrow had run into Balmaseda while taking three donkeys laden with New Testaments around villages in the Segovia area of Old Castile. Borrow, a fine rider himself, whose favourite method of breaking in a young horse was to give it an extra heavy load of Bibles to carry up the flinty lanes of Spain, was apparently impressed by Balmaseda's horsemanship. He records that he saw the Carlist chief come dashing down out of the pinewoods like an avalanche to sack and burn, and that he went on distributing the word of the prophets in the midst of the horrors going on around him.

Borrow made no attempt to assess the character of Balmaseda as he did that of Cabrera while awaiting the never-to-come Carlist assault on Madrid in September 1837. Borrow wrote: 'Cabrera was a dastardly wretch, whose limited mind was incapable of harbouring a single conception approaching to grandeur; whose heroic deeds were confined to cutting down defenceless men and to forcing and disembowelling unhappy women; and yet I have seen this wretched fellow termed in French journals (Carlist of course) the young, the heroic general. Infamy on the cowardly assassin! The shabbiest corporal of Napoleon would have laughed at his generalship, and half a battalion of Austrian grenadiers would have driven him and his rabble army headlong into the Ebro.'

Well, many had tried it and all had failed. George Borrow had also overdone the atrocity stories, doubtless influenced by travellers' tales brought in by refugees from areas pillaged by Cabrera's forces in the countryside outside Madrid. And no less an authority than the Queen Regent's one-time commander of the army of the centre, General Nogueras, would certainly not agree with Borrow's assessment of his generalship, for Nogueras had specifically and officially treated one of Cabrera's feats in Napoleonic analogy. And it is interesting to compare Borrow's impression with that of a French newspaper correspondent three years later. Although the marks of illness were still heavily showing, and the journalist was surprised to see so small a man, he was obviously impressed. Reporting the entry of Cabrera into France, he wrote: 'I have seen Cabrera and it is not to be conceived how so fragile and attenuated a form contains such a determined spirit. But his eye is still brilliant and in seeing him one is convinced that he has within him the germ of some illness which threatens his existence.' The correspondent clearly did not know about Cabrera's breakdown in health, but he had noted the marks.

Cabrera's illness may have been part of the reason why he decided not to stand and fight at Berga with territory favourable to him, for his German biographer, von Rahden, writing immediately after the event, says he was a changed man after it.

Before the Carlist cause began breaking up, Cabrera had been the leader of an army of some 30,000 men and the holder of upwards of thirty forts. He had started out six years before with a mere handful of followers, some of these armed with cudgels cut from the woods because there were not enough muskets to go round. By the end of that first year they had grown to three or four thousand. Then came the build-up to the peak of his immense strength as his personality, his dashing courage and his wounds so endeared him to his men that they would follow him anywhere. Now the faithful remnants had followed him into exile. His name had not merely rung around the world, it had reverberated; and it was to do so again, though perhaps with not so discordant a note.

Looking around at other great guerrilla fighters before and since, some comparison can be made with Mao Tse-tung, who himself, when floundering about in his search for a creed, had a brief flirtation with monarchism, and who, in his fighting days, had suffered agony similar to Cabrera's in that he lost his wife and sister in reprisal executions. The comparison must, however, be in purely military terms, for Cabrera was no revolutionary, left wing or right; he then had no politics, no personal political aims, just a fanatical faith in his own powers of leadership as an instrument for placing Don Carlos on the throne of Spain. Certainly he was not astute enough, as Mao was to show himself to be, to contemplate that political power could come out of the barrel of a gun. Militarily, however, Mao might well have taken lessons from Cabrera, had he ever heard of him, for the Spaniard was almost a century ahead of the Chinese in his thoughts on the latent strength of the peasantry, on recruitment and in the realization that from small guerrilla groups and even bandit gangs grew platoons, companies, regiments, divisions and finally an army. Long before the tags of military opportunist and terrorist were contemptuously hung on Mao, Cabrera was flaunting them brashly and with great success. Equally, the Carlist chief was never short of a thought on how to use execution as an arm to maintain discipline in his own ranks, and to induce support from waverers outside; or on how to obtain intelligence through a network of peasant spies. As to the principles enunciated by Mao in the 1920s – when the enemy advances, retreat; when he halts, harrass him; when he tires, attack; and when he retreats, pursue him – these were the very stuff of Cabrera's tactics in the 1830s, although, unlike Mao, he rarely had a thought for long-term strategy.

As soon as the French authorities had completed their inter-rogation of Cabrera and his staff, they sent him to the old fortress at Ham, on the river Somme in northern France, celebrated for the political prisoners it had housed over the years. Four hundred years earlier Joan of Arc had been held there for a spell. Now it was the turn of Prince Louis Napoleon, who had made a foolish and premature attempt at Boulogne that same year to re-establish Bonaparte imperial rule in France. Ham was wanted for Louis, so Cabrera, after a short time there, was moved farther north to Lille, near the Belgian border. The French had turned down repeated requests from the Spanish government for the extradition of Carlist leaders, but restricted their movements according to their rank and propensities for causing trouble.

Queen Cristina suffered no such restrictions, and was royally received by her uncle, King Louis Philippe, when she reached Paris in November 1840. She was given an apartment in the Palais Royale, took a house for her husband Muñoz, and bought Malmaison, just outside Paris, where the Empress Josephine had set up court after Napoleon had pensioned her off and divorced her.

After her abdication, Cristina had taken ship to France, reaching Port Vendres on the night of 18 October. Three days later, continuing her journey towards Paris, her carriage stopped at the town of Montpellier, where she rested for a few hours at the Hotel du Midi.

Cabrera's health, of which the French newspaper correspondent had taken such a dim view, had deteriorated in the north of France, and the prison medical officer had recommended that he be transferred to the south, to Hyères, on the Mediterranean coast. This was approved by the French authorities, and Cabrera had reached Montpellier and was awaiting onward transport to Hyères, when the coach bearing Maria Cristina towards Paris stopped in the very same place. Cabrera was in the Hotel de Londres only a few paces away from the Midi, and had been in the habit of using the balcony freely during his stay. When the local chief of police learned Cristina was coming, he asked Cabrera to keep off the balcony lest demonstrations be provoked.

The ex-Queen Regent departed for Nîmes at five o'clock in the afternoon. Cabrera, true to his promise, kept off the balcony, but placed himself at a window. Maria Cristina positioned herself at the window of her carriage; and the former queen and her most fanatical adversary over the past seven years looked each other in the face for the first and last time. One report said that she kept her eyes half closed as she passed Cabrera's hotel; another that she smiled on seeing him. If so, it must have been an expression of irony, as must have been Cabrera's answering glance. For Cristina had been forced into exile only three months after Espartero had driven out Cabrera.

When Maria Cristina abdicated, Queen Isabel had only just celebrated her tenth birthday and her other daughter, Luisa, was eight. After bitter disputes with Espartero in Barcelona, Maria Cristina had moved court to Valencia, and her parting there with the royal children on the night of 16 October 1840 was a tearful one. She saw them as they were going to bed, and all three were sobbing and kissing each other, with anxious ladies-in-waiting wringing their hands in the background as she told the two princesses that she must go away. 'Mother, we will go with you,' said the youngest. Maria Cristina fainted in distress. When she recovered, she tried to reassure them by saying she would soon return, and the two children fell into a disturbed sleep. Cristina looked in on them before she set out, but rather than renew their grief let them lie. Her adieu: 'May God and Spaniards render you happy. Love your mother always as she has loved you.' She went away, weeping, to the ship that was to take her to France.

Her farewell to Espartero was dry and bitter. Indignant at

the conduct of the man she had laden with honours, she said: 'You had no reason to complain of me and to treat me thus. I made you successively Count of Luchana, Duke of Victory, Duke of Morella and a Grandee of Spain. The only thing I could not make you was a gentleman.' Safely across the French border, Cristina stopped to issue a manifesto explaining why she had not been able to come to terms with Espartero over the immediate issue, her support for a bill passed by the Cortes to curb the power of the municipalities in Spain. She could not, she said, accept conditions that degraded her own self, acknowledged the right of force, and violated the Constitution. And she declared: 'I saw my sceptre reduced to no more than a useless reed, and my diadem changed into a crown of thorns. My powers were exhausted. In fine, I laid down my sceptre and took off my crown that I might breathe a free air; an unhappy victim but with a calm brow, with a quiet conscience and without any remorse in my soul.'

14

The Queen and the Corporal

There were, of course, those who said that Cristina was only too glad of an excuse to give up, and that she had long been scheming to see how she might leave Spain and live in peace and openly with the man of lowly birth and station for whom she had risked all in a marriage so secret that all the world seemed to get to know about it immediately.

Only a few weeks after the death of her husband Ferdinand, Maria Cristina, still only twenty-seven, became attracted to one of the members of the Garde du Corps, the royal bodyguard. His name, Fernando Muñoz; his rank, corporal; his father, tobacco shop keeper.

Muñoz was about twenty-five years of age, a dashing, handsome soldier (although later portraits show him as a bald, rotund figure), who, it was said, had narrowly escaped dismissal from his regiment a year or so earlier on suspicion of being a supporter of Don Carlos; he left the regiment to join Ferdinand's bodyguard as a young private.

He had frequently caught Cristina's roving eye, and many are the stories of how they first met. There is the inevitable tale of the dropped handkerchief and the doting admirer pressing it fervently to his lips; others of the way Cristina chose to declare herself to the corporal. An account printed by a Madrid journal with access to ministerial information has a ring of truth about it; the journal recorded how Maria Cristina planned a romantic journey for the specific purpose of letting Fernando know of her love for him. The go-betweens were named as the Queen Regent's milliner and confidante, Doña Teresa Valcarcel, and a soldier comrade of Muñoz and friend of Teresa, Nicolas Francia. Muñoz, according to this story, was on guard duty at the palace in the first weeks of December 1833, and Cristina used the opportunity. Although the winter was a severe one, she arranged a coach trip to her country house at Quita Pesares, near the summer palace at La Granja, fifty miles outside Madrid. There were to be four in the party: Cristina; her aide-de-camp, General Palafox; her gentleman usher, Carbonell; and Corporal Muñoz. None of the ladies of the court was allowed to accompany her.

The royal coach set out on 17 December, but broke down while trying to force a passsage through the snowbound mountain road. The party returned to Madrid, where the Queen Regent immediately sent out labourers to clear a way. The coach, with the same four occupants, set out again the next morning and got through to Quita Pesares. There Maria Cristina walked in the gardens with Palafox and Muñoz, but found a pretext to send her aide away so that she could be alone with the corporal of the guard. This, said the journal, was when and where she made her declaration to him. For when they returned to Madrid, the favour enjoyed by the lucky corporal became increasingly evident.

He was appointed Gentleman of the Interior, an office created by the late King, and which observers were quick to remark did not appear seemly for a queen. Cristina presented Fernando with a magnificent house and also allotted him an apartment in the royal palace. Soon he was seen about wearing diamond pins in his cravat and other ornaments of the late King. He dined with the Queen Regent, went everywhere with her, and attended her alone in her carriage, an unusual breach of regal decorum; and they reviewed the National Guard together. This could not, of course, escape the notice of the public, and newspapers made allusions to it. When one, the *Cronica,* recorded that Her Majesty had taken an airing in an open charabanc driven by a servant, the servant alluded to being Muñoz, Cristina took it as an insult, and had the paper suppressed and its two editors exiled.

What, however, the people in the streets did not know, and the editors clearly did, was that the Queen and the corporal were already married.

After returning from Quita Pesares, Maria Cristina had determinedly set about seeing how she could marry Muñoz and at the same time keep the arrangement from the Cortes, whose disapproval would compel her to forfeit the regency and hand over to others the guardianship of the young Queen

Isabel and her other daughter, Luisa. A normal marriage ceremony, apart from the publicity, would mean the publication of banns from the pulpit, so Maria Cristina started pulling strings in order to get a special licence which would obviate this. Several of the Church dignitaries she approached rebuffed her, and she only obtained the licence by writing a personal appeal to her friend Cardinal Tiberi, the papal nuncio.

Then came the difficulty of finding someone to marry them. The story goes that an obscure priest from Fernando's home town of Tarancón, fifty miles from Madrid, happened to be in the capital. Muñoz, by offering him 'advancement', persuaded him to perform the ceremony. So, at seven o'clock in the morning of 28 December 1833, ten days after Quita Pesares and less than three months after the death of King Ferdinand, Doña Maria Cristina de Bourbon, Queen Regent of Spain, and Fernando Muñoz, corporal of the guard, were married in great secrecy by the humble priest from Tarancón, Marcos Antonio Gonzalez. Only two witnesses were present, a Don Miguel Lopez Acabado and the Marquis de Herreros. On 16 November 1834, eleven months after meeting Fernando, Maria Cristina gave birth to a daughter. In the autumn of 1835, a son; later, another son and daughter.

Muñoz's married life was almost cut short in the La Granja mutiny of August 1836, when a group of sergeants, alleged to have been bribed by Mendizábal but more likely acting on their own as senior officials of freemasons' lodges, invaded the summer palace, confronted Maria Cristina and forced her to re-establish the liberal constitution of 1812 which Ferdinand the Desired had abolished only two years after it had been introduced. Muñoz was said to have been insulted, and to have saved his life by hiding in a palace cellar. Queen Cristina was not allowed to go back on her agreement with the sergeants. The 1812 constitution was duly promulgated, and she took pains not to be seen in public with Muñoz so frequently afterwards. Hence the stories in 1840 that she was by no means the reluctant exile.

15
Hero

Soon after Maria Cristina's coach had clattered through the streets of Montpellier to continue her journey to Paris, the walls reverberated with a similar echo as Cabrera's conveyance set out for Hyères. His journey from Lille through Paris to the south, escorted by a chief of the French police, had had something of the nature of a triumphal tour, the French people, Carlist at heart, leaving little room for doubt as to their feelings. In Paris, Cabrera had been closeted at the Hotel d'Orléans, in the rue des Petits Augustins, where he was besieged by callers, leading members of the French aristocracy among them, and fêted every time he appeared in public. In spite of his military defeat and the cruelties and atrocities attached to his name, he was treated as a conquering hero, although many were surprised to find that the terrible Tiger of the Maestrazgo was a smallish man who, naturally or else with consummate affectation, conducted himself in a civil manner and spoke in a quiet voice. Yet Thomas Raikes, writing in his *Journal* in Paris, recorded that one of his friends had seen Cabrera at the French Foreign Office, and had described him as 'a rough peasant'.

People turned out in their hundreds to see him at his many stopping places all the way to the Mediterranean coast. He reached Hyères early in November 1840, and on his pledge that he would not try to escape, was given complete freedom. He continued to hold court, and his stepfather and two surviving sisters joined him. He wintered in Hyères, walking and riding in the mountains or along the coastal paths, and his health improved. But when the equable winter climate gave way to the sweltering heat of summer, he obtained permission to move to Lyons. Here an admiring sympathiser placed a lovely villa with spacious gardens at his disposal and he moved in, his sisters staying with him until it was evident that his health had fully recovered. In these agreeable surroundings, Cabrera received frequent visits from Carlist generals, chiefs and intriguers, as well as from important French legitimists. He corresponded with Don Carlos, who, with his wife and sons, remained under house guard at Bourges in central France.

The years went by and the Spanish political diabolo, twisting and turning in the midst of innumerable bloody riots on the streets of Madrid, spun out Espartero and pulled back Maria Cristina – no more regent it is true, but still to hold considerable sway over Queen Isabel and her court. Espartero went late in 1843, driven out by another military power-seeker, General Narvaez, to receive a warm welcome as a liberal exile in England and to be given the freedom of the City of London and made a Knight Grand Cross of the Order of the Bath. Maria Cristina came back from France early in the following year to frenzied welcomes by the fickle Spanish public, who built triumphal arches for her passage and went to church in their thousands to give thanks for her return.

In Bourges, Don Carlos was pondering what he might do to reactivate the Carlist cause from its long stagnation. In May 1845, after almost five years of enforced inactivity, the Pretender announced that he was abdicating his rights to the Spanish crown to his eldest son, Carlos Luis, then twenty-six.

Meanwhile in Madrid, in order to avoid another military regency after the departure of Espartero, Isabel had been declared of age when she was thirteen and now reigned as queen in her own right. Maria Cristina, having on her return immediately had her clandestine marriage with Muñoz openly confirmed by an official and public ceremony and the former corporal made Duke of Rianzares, was looking around for a husband for her daughter, the Queen.

When, eight years earlier, Don Carlos, waiting nervously yet expectantly at the gates of Madrid, was putting out feelers to those inside, one of his suggestions was that Maria Cristina should agree to the betrothal of Isabel and his son, but always with the reservation that Carlos Luis should be king and not consort. Now he was proposing it again and, to strengthen his proposition, abdicated in favour of his son, who was given the title Count de Montemolin, and became known as Carlos VI. Again, neither father nor son showed any sense of compromise, although they might have achieved most Carlist aims by suggesting that Isabel and Montemolin should share sovereignty. And so, as in 1837, Maria Cristina would have nothing to do with the offer of Carlos Luis' hand; she was not interested in anything that would weaken her daughter's position. Other suitors for Isabel were looked over, with France, England, Austria and Prussia each naming their preferences. In the event, and in the interests of the balance of power in Europe, the husband foisted on the reluctant young queen was her pretty cousin, Francisco Asis, Duke of Cadiz, twenty-four-year-old son of Maria Cristina's forthright sister Carlota – she who had boxed Calomarde's ears.

At the same time a husband was chosen for the Queen's younger sister Luisa; he was the twenty-one-year-old Duke of Montpensier, son of King Louis Philippe of France.

The Queen and her sister, dressed in white lace trimmed with gold, were married in the same hour on the same day, 10 October 1846, with all the pomp and colour of Catholic ceremonial, the Patriarch of the Indies, the highest ecclesiastic, presiding over a bevy of dignitaries and priests. It was Isabel's sixteenth birthday; Luisa was fourteen. Not quite a double wedding: Isabel and Francisco were married first, then Luisa and her French prince, thus technically keeping half the pledge made to England that to ensure Spanish succession Luisa would not marry until the queen had done so, but ignoring the other half which stipulated 'until she had borne children'.

Carlota had not passed on any of her domineering ways to her son, and Isabel, who was to say later that he wore more lace on their wedding night than she did, looked elsewhere for satisfaction. She found a covey of comforting arms, and presented the surprised Francisco with nine children, although it is extremely doubtful that he himself fathered any of them. There were no such questions about the married life of Luisa and Montpensier; at least their four children were born on the right side of the blanket.

Cabrera did not immediately approve of Don Carlos' abdication; he had steadfastly fought for him for seven long

115

years, and as far as Cabrera was concerned Carlos was King of Spain. He soon came to accept it, however, and within a month was writing to declare his support for the new Pretender. When Montemolin eluded the guard at Bourges in September 1846 and escaped to England, rumours about Cabrera began to fly – first that he had joined Montemolin in London, then that he had escaped in a fishing boat and landed in Spain. This latter was published in Madrid as serious information, and the authorities everywhere were told to be on their guard.

Cabrera had in fact not left Lyons, where he was waiting, not too anxiously, for his master's voice. It was a long time coming. True, Montemolin issued a manifesto or two and, after Isabel's marriage, a proclamation restating his rights to the throne. But the twenty-eight-year-old count seemed to be enjoying his free-living exile in London where he had built up a reputation in the social whirl as a lover of music and an accomplished dancer.

Cabrera's not uncomfortable style in Lyons was working a change in him, too, and he almost turned a deaf ear to the call when it did come, which was not until the spring of 1848. In Catalonia over the previous eighteen months, Carlist bands had been waging sporadic warfare in the so-called Matiners (or Earlyrisers) War – something along the lines of the early guerrilla raids in Aragon in 1833. Now with revolution sweeping Europe, King Louis Philippe overthrown in France, and continual intrigue, blood and confusion in Madrid, the Carlist advisers thought anew that, given a show of strength, the people of Spain might yet rise up in support of their man. So Montemolin's message to Cabrera was: Go and pull these forces and actions together and raise my standard in Catalonia. You are appointed supreme commander of the operation.

Cabrera received the order with diffidence, if not outright repugnance, for he was a changing character after seven years of exile. He put forward, for him, the surprising argument that Spain badly needed a long period of peace. Nevertheless he accepted Montemolin's command, although he added: 'I go because honour and decorum demand it. But I have a presentiment that all these hopes will be frustrated.' So on

23 June 1848, eight years after he had been evicted, Cabrera descended the Pyrenees and re-entered Spain to fight again for God, Country and King; the second Carlist war was in motion.

News of his re-entry created a sensation throughout Spain, but in terms of expression only; for again there was no popular rising, and Montemolin's advisers were proved as wrong as his father's had been in advocating the royal marches eleven years earlier. On his arrival in Catalonia Cabrera found a few ill-armed groups of doubtful allegiance. But, drawing on his experience, and travelling about the country sometimes disguised as a priest, he welded them together into a force of some 10,000 men, which for a time held in check Government forces five times that number. But disagreements broke out and defections occurred, and it was all over within ten months. As before, he needed a strong fortress – a Catalan Morella or Cantavieja – to serve as his base. But his attempts to surprise fortified towns were unfruitful, and this time there were no fifth columnists inside to throw open the gates. At first Government troops failed to catch up with his divisions, but ceaseless military activity on the part of a new commander, General Concha, combined with the gold and pardons offered to those who deserted the Carlist ranks, soon had him on the run; while heavy Government taxes on places which had harboured his troops made it increasingly difficult to find sustenance. He made his last big stand at Pasteral, on the banks of the River Ter, a battle for which Montemolin was to award him the highest military rank, captain general, and make him a marquis – for memorable deeds, he said, worthy to be transmitted to posterity in indelible characters. Cabrera's men put up a good fight against very much stronger forces, but the battle came to a premature end when he was hit in the thigh by a musket ball and was hurried away wounded into the snow-covered hills. There he was saved from capture only by the loyalty and diversionary tactics of the few men remaining with him. Before he was fully recovered, some of the old fire rose up in him, and he went back into the fray; but soon his forces had to abandon the line of the Ter, and he himself came very near to capture again.

Carlos VI, Count Montemolin, son of the first Carlist Pretender . . . a flattering portrait disguising the bent nose and the 'Bourbon eye'.

Cabrera had entered the Matiners War full of pessimism, yet at the same time resolved not to repeat the mistakes of old. A changed man in many ways, he no longer spoke of the absolute rule of King and Church; on the contrary, and looking at the misrule and scandals of the court in Madrid, he urged that Spain needed true liberty – a word that was anathema to hard-line Carlists, who looked at him with

118

renewed suspicion. Primarily, Cabrera had decided to wage a humane war, to abandon his old methods of terrorism and reprisal. But the cruelty, though suppressed, was not far from the surface; it could, said one observer, still be seen in his eyes, and in the end it welled up and overwhelmed him. With senior officers taking their pieces of silver and deserting around him, and his mind heavy with the fear of assassination – so much so, it was said, that he took to wearing metal-lined leather trousers and a shirt of mail – he fell back into his old ways. His raiding parties made short work of any deserter who happened to fall into their hands. Then, increasingly hard-pressed by General Concha and with no light anywhere on his horizon, he added one final black spot to his already heavily blotted book.

A local landowner, Baron de Abella, got some of his friends together with the idea that if they could induce the Carlists to see that their cause was lost and that nothing could be gained by continuing the struggle, they might get them to lay down their arms and save a lot of unnecessary bloodshed. He got in touch with one of Cabrera's deputies, Rafael Tristany, whose family he knew, believing it to be useless to approach Cabrera himself. Tristany informed Cabrera, who set a trap. He got Tristany to arrange a meeting with the baron and two of his companions, whereupon he delivered them up to his chief, who had them shot. Cabrera argued that Abella was an agent of the Madrid Government, out to get him, or at least to seduce his officers; but the baron was a much respected man in the area, and there is no doubt that he acted from sincere and humane, if not completely disinterested motives. With the fact obvious that Cabrera's forces had been disintegrating around him, and that they had no hope of success, this act raised a public outcry almost as great as that which followed his reprisal shootings of women hostages at Valderrobres in the first Carlist war.

Cabrera himself knew the end of the campaign was near. Then he was surprised in the very place where the baron and his friends had been handed over to the executioner. A column led by one of his former brigadiers, named Pons, who had gone over to General Concha's forces, and whose brother Cabrera had then had shot, encircled the town. Again, it was

Pasteral, Cabrera's last battle. He lost it and went into exile but it gained him another title, Marquis del Ter.

only diversionary tactics, this time by an officer who caused confusion in the Government ranks, which allowed Cabrera and a handful of men to gallop furiously through their lines and into the mountains, where he was kept holed up as some of his chiefs and men sought refuge in France. Concha chased the dispersed Cabrera forces, and captured one of his most loyal and trusted commanders, who had fought under the *nom de guerre* Marsal, right from the beginning of the Matiners War. He was condemned to death, but pardoned on making a loyal submission to the Queen.

Before this, in the midst of the defections and with everything in disarray, Cabrera got a message through to Montemolin in London appealing to him to present himself in person on the battlefield, and perhaps reanimate the flagging spirits of the partisans. When the message reached London, the Pretender had just become engaged to an English girl. Nevertheless, he packed his bags and left. He crossed

France, but the French police were waiting, still carrying his description issued at the time he fled Bourges: Age, 28; height, 5ft 5ins; hair, beard and eyebrows, black; forehead, narrow and prominent; face, oval and dark-skinned; eyes, brown. It was blunt enough to describe the nose as large, long, and slightly twisted, the teeth as a little prominent, 'particularly when he speaks', and to remark on the Bourbon squint. The police stopped Montemolin near the Spanish border and escorted him back to the nearest French town. He returned to London to face up to the problems of love, not war. There were some who said that it was all a hoax and that he never left – a story to this effect appeared in some English and Continental newspapers; others that the French police had been tipped off by members of his court overfond of the fleshpots of London life. The evidence is, however, that he did make the attempt. Betrayal or not, in Catalonia it was the end, and on 23 April 1849, precisely ten months after he had entered Spain, Cabrera recrossed the Pyrenees for a second exile in France. This time he was taken to the fortress of La Malgue in Toulon.

16

Battle of Words

Even before Cabrera had left Spain the first time, the pens of Spanish historians and biographers had been gliding over reams of virgin paper in praise or condemnation of the Carlist general and his exploits. By the time he was driven out again in 1849, novelists and poets had joined in, to send a stream of books flowing through the Spanish presses. One of the first books to appear, however, was in German, from the pen of Wilhelm Baron von Rahden, a soldier of royal fortunes who had served for twenty-five years in the Royal Prussian and Royal Netherlands Armies, taking part in campaigns in Germany, France and Belgium. He had then offered his services to 'the legitimate royal house of Spain'. He was in fact the brigadier in charge of Cabrera's engineers who had organized Morella's defences in preparation for Espartero's assault. On a plea of ill health, he moved out before the attack, and was back in Frankfurt writing his assessment of Cabrera and the war almost before it had ended.

Von Rahden said the personal character of Cabrera had never been properly understood because the 'liberal press', particularly in Spain and France, had held back the truth or deliberately lied. There was no doubt about Cabrera's ability as a soldier and a general; but he was a completely different person after his illness, when his actions had laid themselves open to criticism. Von Rahden claimed to know Cabrera well; inevitably they must have had frequent contact, and the book contains the facsimile of a signed note from Cabrera (dated 19 November 1839, just before his illness) and a portrait. But von Rahden, in his references to the execution of Cabrera's mother, is so inaccurate that one must take his account of Cabrera's career with some reserve. As has already been said, pick where you will among the Cabrera literature, and you will come up with a different age for his mother when she was shot. Von Rahden, though writing little more than three years after the event, takes the prize. He said she was seventy-two, blind and lame. She was fifty-three – 53 years 2 months and 19 days as Cabrera's early biographer and friend Buenaventura Cordoba precisely put it, born 28 November 1872 – and she walked unaided to her place of execution.

As the years went by, more Spanish writers joined the throng, mainly with eulogistic biographies, while poets versified his actions in songs of praise. But two mid-nineteenth century literary gentlemen, Wenceslao Ayguals and Rafael Gonzalez, found themselves squabbling in print. Ayguals wrote a book denouncing Cabrera and dwelling on the atrocity stories; Gonzalez followed immediately with a book of refutation. Ayguals put out a second edition, Gonzalez a second refutation. Ayguals dedicated his book to his brother Joaquim, one of the young men of Vinaroz butchered by Cabrera's guerrillas in 1835. Ayguals said that Joaquim, a captain of militia, had been cowardly assassinated, with sixty-two other young men of Vinaroz, by the ferocious Cabrera. Altars had been set up to a spurious Spaniard – a monster who was an executioner of the innocent and murderer of heroic soldiers after the fight was over – and he, Ayguals, had been compelled to put the record straight. Ridiculous importance had been given to Cabrera's supposed talents, for he was nothing more than a bandit leader who had fanned simple controversy into flames, a hyena whose cruelties were comparable to those of Nero and Caligula in Rome; Judge Jefferies and his Bloody Assize in Britain; and Carrier, a French revolutionary whose pet method of getting rid of his prisoners was to ship them out into the Loire aboard vessels with trapdoors in the hulls, through which they were dropped into the muddy depths of the river. Among the whole tribes of darkest Africa could not be found a catalogue of crimes so dreadful.

As to the apologist view that Cabrera's bestiality stemmed from the death of his mother, said Ayguals, this was demonstrably false, for before her death Cabrera himself had perpetrated the assassination of more than one hundred inoffensive persons and soldiers who had surrendered. Far from meriting songs of praise, this dissolute bandit and seducer deserved only universal execration. Gonzalez, in his refutation, sarcastically mimicked Ayguals' dedication and said his book was libellous and immoral, written with rancour because of the death of his brother, who with many unfortunate militiamen of Vinaroz 'died in battle' with the forces of Cabrera. If he died in fight, Gonzalez said, he was not assassinated by the Caudillo of Tortosa; it could only be said that he was a victim of his own bravery.

Articles in the press of northern Europe, where Austria and Prussia had supported Don Carlos from the beginning, were laudatory, and there were widespread though not universal tributes in France. There was a Carlist faction in Britain, and one of its leading advocates was *Blackwood's Magazine*. In following the war, *Blackwood's* had treated the Carlists of the north as worthy upholders of a legitimate claim, and denounced the British Government for sending ships, men and supplies to the Queen of Spain's forces. But when the magazine looked at the eastern theatre it turned on Cabrera in scathing denunciation. Introducing in September 1846 a lengthy review of a book on the war in Aragon and Valencia by three Spanish writers, one of whom had been a leading Cristino official in Teruel province during the fighting and so obviously not an unbiased observer, *Blackwood's* had this to say: 'Our intention, six years after, is not to rake over details of the war, but to give a correct notion of the character of a man who by one party has been extolled as a hero, by another stigmatised as a savage . . . From the day that Cabrera assumed the command, the war became a butchery and its inflictions ceased to be confined to the armed combatants on either side. Thenceforward the infant in the cradle, the bedridden old man, the pregnant matron were included amongst its victims. A mere suspicion of liberal opinions, the possession of a national guardsman's uniform, a glass of water given to a wounded Cristino, a distant relationship to a partisan of the Queen, was sentence of death. The rules of civilised warfare were set at nought and Cabrera, in obedience to his sanguinary instincts, committed his murders not only when they might possibly advance, but even when they must positively injure, the cause of him whom he styled his sovereign. "Those days that I do not shed blood," said he in July 1837, when waiting in the ante-chamber of Don Carlos with other Carlist generals, "I have not a good digestion." During the five years of his command his digestion can rarely have been troubled.'

Thus spake the magazine that had been the uninhibited supporter of the Carlist campaign in the north; and it had no hesitation in going on to quote the book's partisan description of the fighters in the east. 'They were the dregs and refuse of the population,' it said. 'Highwaymen, smugglers, escaped criminals, profligate monks, bad characters of every description, banded together under chiefs little better than themselves . . . The clergy played a conspicuous part. Scarce one of the rebel leaders but had his clerical staff of chaplains, sharing, often stimulating, his cruelties and excesses. The most subversive sermons were preached; the confessional became the vehicle of insidious and treasonable admonitions; the liberal section of the clergy was subjected to cruel molestation and injustice. All this added to the scandal and discord that reigned in the convents . . . in a rebellion so enthusiastically shared in and promoted by the monks.'

Not long before this *Blackwood's* article, Wenceslao Ayguals had put out in Madrid the first edition of his book, to mark the tenth anniversary of his brother's death, when the young men of Vinaroz went to help their neighbours at Alcanar. He must have been surprised, and his refuter Rafael Gonzalez discomfited, to find a pro-Carlist magazine giving a fair measure of support for his own assessment of Cabrera, though admittedly, as Gonzalez was at pains to point out, this must have been coloured by the way his brother met his untimely end.

Two and a half years later, however, *Blackwood's* was describing Cabrera in more kindly terms when taking stock of the Matiners War. In this, it said, mercy and humanity were his device, and he aimed to win followers by clemency and conciliation, adding this personal picture: 'He is neither ugly nor handsome. He has neither assassin-scowl nor an expression like a bilious hyena, nor any other of the little physiognomical *agréments* with which imaginative painters have so frequently embellished his countenance. His character, as well as his face, has suffered from misrepresentation. He has been depicted as a Nero on a small scale dividing his time between fiddling and massacre. There is some exaggeration in this statement. Unquestionably, he is neither mild nor merciful; he has shed much blood and has been guilty of diverse acts of cruelty, but more of these have been attributed to him than ever committed.'

17
Tiger Tamed

Cabrera did not stay long in France this time. When it was clear that he had no intention of resuming the war in Spain the French released him and he went to England. The Carlist commander-in-chief joined Montemolin in London and was a sought-after guest at dinner parties, dances and receptions that Carlist sympathisers among the aristocracy gave for the Pretender.

Both Cabrera and Montemolin were to get caught up in serious affairs of the heart. Before Cabrera had called him to Spain, Montemolin had fallen head over heels for a fetching young lady in London, a twenty-three-year-old socialite named Adeleine de Horsey, and they became engaged just before he made his abortive attempt to answer Cabrera's appeal. When the Pretender was sent back by the French police, he announced that he was abdicating his rights to his younger brother, Juan, to meet Carlist objections to the marriage. Don Juan showed no disposition at all to put on the mantle of Pretender, and solemnly burned his brother's letter; which turned out to be very sensible seeing that almost immediately sweet Adeleine, disenchanted with the change of status implicit in abdication, broke off the engagement, and Montemolin was happy to resume the role.

His commander-in-chief's romance was to prove more lasting. At one of the London receptions Cabrera met the wealthy daughter of a QC landowner of Welsh ancestry, Robert Vaughan Richards, who had died and left his vast fortune to her, his only child. The Tiger of the Maestrazgo had met his tigress! Her name was Marianne Catherine. Despite differences in age, religion and background, they were married on 29 May 1850, within a year of the Carlist general leaving Spain. Cabrera was then forty-three, his bride twenty-nine.

Cabrera's English home at Wentworth, where Carlist kings and plotters used to tread and where putters now click to lesser battles.

Marianne being a Protestant, there were two ceremonies. At the first, at the Roman Catholic chapel in Spanish Place, Manchester Square, Don Juan was best man, bringing with him Montemolin's wedding present, the additional title of Marquis del Ter (after the recent battle of Pasteral on the banks of the River Ter), and his new military rank, Captain-General of the Carlist Armies. At the Protestant ceremony at the fashionable St George's, Hanover Square, conducted by the Revd Temple Frere, Canon of Westminster, Don Juan gave way to Lord John Manners, MP.

The Illustrated London News referred to a bevy of young ladies attending the bride and to an elegant *dejeuner* after the ceremony, not forgetting to add that the fair lady was reputed to have a fortune of £25,000 a year, a point that *The Gentleman's Magazine* also found interesting. The honeymoon was spent neither in Spain (unlikely in any event) nor France; they went to Tunbridge Wells.

Meanwhile, his king, the Count Montemolin, had forgotten his affaire with Adeleine de Horsey and married within his station – his bride Princess Carolina of Naples, another of the many sisters of Maria Cristina and Carlota. He went off to live there, while Don Carlos, the Princess de Beira, and his

130

youngest son Fernando, freed from exile in France, established their court in Trieste, Don Carlos having named himself Count of Molina, one of the many titles of the Spanish crown.

The Cabreras, or the Count and Countess of Morella as they preferred to be known, spent the first few years of their married life in London at Eaton Square, where there was a Richards house. They then moved to Virginia Water and set up house in the many acred mansion that is now the clubhouse of the Wentworth Golf Club. They spent the rest of their lives there; and there, it seems, the Tiger of the Maestrazgo was tamed. He had clearly met his match in Marianne Catherine; and there was the soothing impact of her fortune and the gentleman's life that went with it, as well as the caress of the English countryside.

In London and Wentworth, the magic of his name still strong, Cabrera had frequent visits from Carlist emissaries and conspirators, received the successive Pretenders themselves, and engaged in lengthy correspondence with them. He himself made numerous journeys to Continental capitals, sometimes accompanied by his wife who, though not a convert to the Carlist cause, made financial contributions to it along with her husband. But Cabrera's enthusiasm for militant Carlism, which had already shown signs of waning in Lyons ten years earlier, became less and less as the experience of true Liberalism and the comforts of English country life influenced his own thinking.

In Madrid the political diabolo had another amazing twirl in 1854, precisely reversing its act of 1840, pulling back Espartero and evicting the returned Maria Cristina, who with her husband, the one-time corporal now Duke of Rianzares, had long been accused of using her position to make private fortunes out of railway and other public works contracts as the country was opened up, and fortunate now to escape with their lives as the mob ransacked their house.

Maria Cristina, now a roundly matron, yet still able to put on the regal style, was not to return to Spain again, and she spent the next twenty years of her life in exile, dying near Le Havre in France in 1878 at the age of seventy-two. Muñoz, the corporal duke, had died five years earlier.

O'Donnell, the general who had helped Espartero to defeat Cabrera, and who had chosen exile with Maria Cristina in 1840, had returned to rise to supreme power, but could not save her this time. It was, in fact, his move against corrupt ministers around the throne of Isabel that had unintentionally brought the mobs on to the streets, and ironically secured the return of Espartero, for O'Donnell then had to play second fiddle to the Duke of Victory. As they worked together to bring order to the chaotic political scene, and curb the excesses and indiscretions of Isabel's private life, the Carlists in the traditional 'royalist' areas took advantage of the situation.

The Carlists rose up in several districts, but the risings soon petered out or were put down, and Cabrera had nothing to do with them. He also looked on from London when Montemolin made one last fling to get into Spain, and succeeded only in meeting disaster. On 2 April 1860, at a time when the bulk of the Spanish army was in Morocco, the Pretender and his brother Fernando, with the veteran Carlist General Elio and a few other staff officers, landed on the beach at San Carlos de le Rapita, where Cabrera had acquired the boats with which to take the Royal Expedition across the Ebro. They came with a force of no more than 3500 men brought from the Balearic Islands by the captain-general there, Ortega, recently converted to Carlism by, of all people, Carlota, who had turned her coat after a bitter quarrel with her sister Maria Cristina. This time, many people in high places had been bought, underpinning the still constant Carlist hope that there would be popular risings in favour of the Pretender. But, as in the past, no one stirred. The Spanish people did not even have the option, for the landing was a complete fiasco, and as a military operation it never started.

General Ortega, who, in his own words, had resolved 'to perform some great and bold deed in which he would lose his life or make his name famous', must take the blame for this. He did not tell his troops the purpose of their voyage; when they found out on landing that they were involved in a Carlist plot to seize the throne, they cheered Isabel instead of the Pretender, and refused to continue. As Ortega was

132

haranguing them, his horse took hold of the bit and ran away with him. He might as well have let the sagacious animal take him where it willed, for when he reined it in and brought it back he could make no impression on his men, and in the end had to ride hard over Cabrera's old mountain stronghold of the Maestrazgo to a place where he hoped to hide in the house of a friend. Ill-luck chased folly, for his friend was not at home, and Ortega was arrested and taken to Tortosa, where he was tried by a military court composed of officers junior in rank to him, and therefore, he argued, incompetent to judge him. They brushed aside his plea and condemned him, allowing him to achieve both his aims – fame and death. On 21 April he was executed in the place where Cabrera's mother had faced the firing squad fourteen years earlier.

On the same day Montemolin, Fernando and Elio were discovered not far from Tortosa, in a house where they had been hiding for more than two weeks. They, too, were brought to Cabrera's birthplace. They were luckier than Ortega. Queen Isabel, doubtless fearful that important people would be named and the delicate political balance further upset if there were a trial, graciously allowed them to go free after Montemolin and Fernando had each signed an abject renunciation of their claims to the throne.

Their actions horrified true legitimists everywhere, despite the fact that Montemolin and Fernando retracted the Tortosa renunciation as soon as they were safely back in exile; these rights, their critics declared, were divine rights and could not be surrendered. Cabrera, who had tried to dissuade Montemolin from the landing, arguing among other things that at least 20,000 loyal men were needed to give any chance of success, was not surprised at the outcome. He himself had taken pains to show that he was having nothing to do with the landing by parading up and down Regent Street during the early days of April, making sure that he was seen, particularly by members of the Spanish community in London.

Don Juan, who had burned his brother Montemolin's letter of abdication during the Miss de Horsey affaire, now took the Tortosa renunciation seriously, so that for a time there were two Pretenders. Within nine months, however, both

Rare photographs of Cabrera and his countess, the heiress

Montemolin and Fernando, and Montemolin's wife Carolina, were lying dead in Trieste. They had been taken ill while visiting Carolina's sister, the Duchess de Berry, at her lakeside home in the Austrian province of Styria, just north of Trieste. Fernando died there and they brought his body back

Marianne Catherine Richards, at Wentworth in their middle years.

to Trieste, where a few days later, on 13 January 1861, Montemolin and Carolina passed away within hours of each other. The inevitable rumours of foul play by poisoning were freely circulating, but the most likely cause of death was cholera or typhus. All were buried beside the first Don

Carlos, who had died in Trieste on 10 March 1855 at the age of sixty-seven, Cabrera and the Countess of Morella making the long journey from London to attend his funeral.

It was in 1855 that the Cabreras moved to Wentworth. The general had not, and did not, let the comings and goings of Carlist kings and advisers, or his voluminous correspondence, interfere with his enjoyment of English country life. He joined his wife in the hunting field, and the late S. F. A. Coles, who wrote the first full biography of General Franco, has an intriguing sidelight on this. Franco, questioned about fear in an interview with Coles, clothed his answer in a reference to the Carlist general. 'Cabrera went in for foxhunting,' Franco remarked, 'but it was noticed by other riders that he always avoided taking gates or hedges and would lead his mount away in search of easier exits. One day a hard-riding English-woman asked him if he was afraid to jump the natural obstacles at a hunt. Cabrera replied: "*Señora, tengo miedo solamente de una cosa, morir sin gloria.*" (Lady, I fear only one thing, to die without glory – to die a foolish death.) 'A very Spanish attitude,' commented the interpreter at the interview, and Franco nodded his head in agreement.

Whether this attitude was uppermost in Cabrera's mind when Carlos VII, son of his best man Don Juan, offered him command of Carlist forces for yet another military campaign is not clear. But if he had been dubious in 1848, now he was clearly faltering.

Montemolin's death in 1861 had solved the immediate problem of the two Pretenders; but the survivor, Juan, second son of Carlos V, showed little leadership, offended the traditionalists by expressing liberal sentiments, and at one time had gone so far as to recognize Isabel as Queen. Carlism was seven years in these doldrums as its leaders searched their minds and their hearts and looked for a more suitable candidate. All this time Don Carlos' widow, the imperious Princess de Beira, had, from her home in Trieste, been keeping a distant but calculating eye on the upbringing of Juan's eldest son – another Carlos – and she now publicly espoused his candidature. Juan had two sons, and soon after the birth of the second had separated from his wife, Princess Beatrix, leaving her to bring them up – first at Modena in

Italy, then in Prague and Venice. The mother did her best to keep her sons from getting mixed up in Carlism, and when in 1861 Cabrera and his wife went to Prague to see them she turned them away. Nevertheless, some of Carlos' tutors saw to it that he knew Carlist aims and history and learned about the heroic figures such as Zumalacárregui and Cabrera who had helped to make it. The boy's appetite whetted, the Princess de Beira developed it, and soon he became desperately keen to play his part.

Five years later Cabrera met him at Innsbruck in an encounter engineered by the princess, when Carlos was eighteen and the general sixty. The meeting was not a success; Carlos was shaken to find that the famous Tiger of the Maestrazgo, about whom he had heard so much, was a cautious old gentleman, neither English nor Spanish, as he was to later describe him.

Cabrera, for his part, could have had nothing but admiration for the young man, although their subsequent relations were to be very difficult. For after a succession of diffident, unhappy, unhandsome leaders, here was one who looked every inch a king – six feet tall, graceful as well as handsome, with the light of decision in his eyes. Few could fault him, and he became acceptable to Carlists everywhere; in July 1868 a Grand Carlist Council was summoned to meet in London, and the twenty-year-old prince was publicly proclaimed Carlos VII, his father Juan eventually accepting the position in a formal abdication. Juan did this at the moment when Queen Isabel, after a troubled and unwise reign that nevertheless had lasted thirty-five years, if her mother's regency is included, had been forced off the throne and into exile in France. 'I thought I had struck deeper roots in this land,' she said resignedly as she bowed out to a military coup led by General Serrano (one of her first lovers), General Prim (who had made a strange approach to Cabrera in London) and Admiral Topete, commander of the Spanish Atlantic squadron.

Don Juan went to live in Brighton, where he found a comforting anonymity that stayed with him right up to his death there in November 1887 at the age of sixty-five. A few months later his body was taken to Trieste to lie in the vault of Carlist Pretenders; at the same time Maria Francisca, first wife of the first Don Carlos, was disinterred, after lying buried at Gosport for fifty years, and taken home with him.

Prim, in his curious approach to Cabrera, had not of course offered him the Spanish crown. He had wanted to know, however, if Cabrera was prepared to use his influence to persuade the Carlists to join the liberal-progressives in Spain in the move to dethrone Isabel, and he had sent an emissary to Wentworth at the end of 1867 to sound him out. A similar approach had been made direct to Carlos VII. Although it seemed a possibility that Cabrera might have moved far enough to accept liberal principles, he was not yet ready to make an alliance with his old enemies, and Prim's man went away empty-handed.

The new Pretender, Carlos VII, established his court in Paris, where he and his generals started planning for a new campaign. Cabrera, his attitude to Carlism changing fast, had exchanged many letters with Carlos, and the old Carlist chief did not attend the London Council, although a seat was kept vacant for him during the whole of its deliberations. It was probably not a deliberate refusal, although it may well be that, given his changing attitudes, he found the illness that kept him in bed at Wentworth very convenient. He was still the great man, the brilliant general, the legendary figure, in the minds of all Carlists, whatever their rank, so much so that when in the following year Don Carlos decided that the moment for action had come, he was obliged to invite Cabrera to become his commander-in-chief. The Pretender had been to Wentworth to see him when he did not turn up at the London Council; now he sent emissaries there to convey his offer. They found a reluctant candidate. First of all Cabrera refused on the grounds of health and age – he was now sixty-two – then he accepted on certain conditions, chief among which was that he himself would name the time and place of any new military operation.

Fighting broke out in a number of areas in uncoordinated risings, and Don Carlos himself was inveigled into entering Spain; but it turned out to be no more than a token crossing of the French frontier, for when he got there the promised rising had not materialized and he had no force to lead.

Cabrera, furious at what he considered a foolhardy move, and arguing that his conditions had been broken, immediately withdrew. The Pretender persuaded him to reconsider, but there was a further difficult and ever-deteriorating series of exchanges, with Cabrera pressing for a Carlist policy manifesto that would offer Spain a liberal constitution and a constitutional monarchy with the Church independent – near blasphemy in the ears of the Carlist intransigents. A discussion between them at Bad Ems in Germany became so bitter that Don Carlos, convinced that Cabrera was defecting, said afterwards: 'The day my cause triumphs my first charge will be to shoot Cabrera.' The general got to hear about this and he then submitted his resignation in writing.

Don Carlos had now moved from Paris to Switzerland, and at Vevey he summoned another grand council to consider the situation. This council, attended by almost a hundred generals, bishops, grandees and suchlike, endorsed the Pretender's proposal that he should take over complete military and party leadership himself. There was a vociferous section calling for instant military action, but they lost the day and it was decided first of all to try constitutional action in Spain, a move somewhat in Cabrera's direction. Serrano, now acting as regent, and Prim, the Prime Minister, although they had pushed Isabel off the throne, were seeking to restore the monarchy with a more democratic and less controversial incumbent. It was like the search for a bridegroom for Isabel some twenty-five years before all over again, with much the same antagonists, in the shape of the major powers, making much the same pressures and objections. As in the case of the royal marriage, so now the various candidates were eliminated or chose to withdraw their hand. In the end, Prim's royal roulette picked out an Italian, Prince Amadeo, second son of King Victor Emmanuel. He entered Madrid as king in the first days of January 1871, only to find that Prim, his patron, had been assassinated. Amadeo did his sincere best to rule an unruleable country, but soon retired despondent and defeated.

In the meantime, the Carlist political approach had got off to a good start, Carlist supporters winning about sixty seats in the Cortes; but in the new elections in the following year –

almost certainly rigged – they lost a third of them. The hawks around the Pretender devoured the signal, and Carlists everywhere were again called to arms. Elio, faithful general of three Pretenders and now in his seventies, became Don Carlos' Minister of War and chief adviser.

Carlos VII entered Spain on 2 May, calling on people everywhere to rise and fight for *Dios, Fueros, Patria,* with the emphasis on regional autonomy and medieval political theory – a subtle change from the 'God, Country, King' of his predecessors. The Third Carlist War had begun. The Pretender announced: 'I am coming to encourage the brave, hearten the lukewarm, and strike terror into traitors.' He incurred a disastrous initial defeat and only narrowly escaped capture, but came back the following year to lead a campaign which overall lasted nearly four years. At Guernica, on the spot where the great oak had been destroyed by the French, he swore to uphold the ancient privileges of the Basques. Although this time the Carlists were fighting a foreign king, and later, when Amadeo abdicated in February 1873, a republic, and everything was thus in their favour, the war in the end achieved as little as its forerunners, though the Carlists had many early successes and one great glory which they commemorate annually to this day – the defeat of the republican forces at Estella in 1874 in the shadow of the Carlist holy mountain Montejurra – a battle in which General Concha, the man who had driven Cabrera out of Catalonia, was killed.

The old, old mistakes were repeated: a new siege of Bilbao, as tempting yet as unsuccessful as the first; failure to press home an attack when within striking distance of Madrid; unrequited hopes of a universal rising in their favour; excesses and atrocities by some of the Carlist troops. The final result was as before: collapse and defeat after the Basques had, again, secured their *fueros* in a negotiated agreement with the government commander.

Cabrera, the fire and ferocity of his youth burned out, wanted and played no part in this war. But the last act on the Carlist stage was largely his. At Sandhurst at that time was a young Spanish cadet, Alfonso Francisco de Bourbon. He was the only son of Queen Isabel, his reputed father an army

Cabrera, the 'English' country patriarch.

captain Puig Molto, although Isabel's patient husband Francisco freely accepted paternity. After she was driven out of Spain, towards the end of 1868, Isabel had named Alfonso Prince of the Asturias, the legitimate heir to the throne; now there was a determined move in Spain to seat him on it.

Cabrera had seen the young Sandhurst cadet at Wentworth, and it was from the military college that he was called home to be king. On 1 December 1874 Alfonso signed a declaration, the so-called Sandhurst Manifesto, in which he expressed his faith in the hereditary monarchy and declared himself a good Catholic and a true liberal, things that had hitherto been incompatible in Spanish court and political life. Cabrera supported the manifesto, and advised Carlists to change their tactics and try peaceful persuasion – which, but for the gradual and perceptible change in him, would have been an unbelievable volte-face for this man.

The Sandhurst cadet, then seventeen, entered Madrid in mid-January 1875 as King Alfonso XII, to the typical scenes of wild rejoicing which the Madrileños seemed capable of bestowing so generously and impartially on all royal comers, irrespective of origin or intent.

Then in March, after negotiations in Paris at the Hotel Mirabeau in the rue de la Paix with a delegation Alfonso had sent from Madrid, Cabrera announced his recognition of the young King, and urged all Carlists to do the same. In this Parisian Embrace, he signed an agreement reminiscent of Vergara, guaranteeing the Basques and the Navarrese their *fueros*, and the retention by Carlists who followed his example of their ranks and titles; and he who had named Maroto traitor now found himself so named.

The news caused consternation in the Carlist camp. The Carlists could not believe their ears, and they heaped abuse and ridicule on their former hero, who became an object of hatred and contempt. Carlos VII and his forces were still in Spain, and from his headquarters at Durango he issued a decree branding Cabrera a traitor, and ordering him to be stripped of all his titles, rank and decorations. The old tiger may have lost his teeth, but his tongue could still lash out. 'You may take away the crosses and titles I have won with my blood,' he retorted immediately. 'I keep the scars that represent them. God and history will judge your Highness' conduct and mine.' He did not lose his titles, for a grateful King Alfonso confirmed them for Cabrera and his descendants for all time so that he remained Conde de Morella, Marquis del Ter, and became a Marshal of Spain, while his countess received the Grand Cross of the Royal Order of Maria Louisa.

Alfonso's accession was the deathblow to the hopes and

desires of Carlos VII. His troops had long been on the retreat, and, after defeat by General Primo de Riviera at Estella, he crossed into France on the last day of February 1876, never to set foot in Spain again. The Carlist wars were over, although there were many who looked upon the civil war sixty years later as nothing more than another Carlist struggle, a new battle against the hated liberals; certainly the red-bereted *Requetés* played no mean part in General Franco's victory over the republican forces.

The great powers and the Pope recognized Alfonso, and in Spain large sections of the clergy, hitherto the strongest of Carlist supporters, rallied to his throne, while a number of senior Carlist officers followed Cabrera's lead. Carlos VII, driven into exile as his predecessors had been, became a wanderer, embarrassing the governments in some of the countries where he stayed. No caustic comment on his defeat or on Cabrera's defection could come from the grand old lady of Carlism, the Princess de Beira, though doubtless she was turning in the grave that had received her in Trieste two years before at the age of eighty-one. But she would have approved Carlos' refusal to surrender his claims to the Spanish crown. He took no more violent action to press them, however, and he died at Varese in Italy in July 1909, aged sixty-one, leaving a son, Jaime, to carry on the tradition.

18

Family Man

Despite Balmaseda's talk about millions brought out at the end of the first Carlist war, Cabrera did not give the impression of being a rich man when he landed in England in 1849. But Marianne Catherine was a very rich consort. She had just inherited her father's considerable fortune, and brought into the marriage a country estate in Wales as well as property in England. Five children were born of the marriage. The first was a girl, Maria Teresa Luisa, then a son, named Ramón after his father – both born before the Cabreras set up house at Wentworth. Then, at Wentworth, came two more boys, Ferdinand and Leopold, and finally another daughter, Ada.

The second son, Ferdinand, following a little in the foot-steps of his father, went to Germany and took a commission in the German army. He became commander of the Prussian Dragoon Guards, and the Emperor Wilhelm II made him his Master of Ceremonies. Ferdinand was still serving the Kaiser in this position when he died in September 1914, just as World War I was beginning. He had not married, and died intestate leaving an estate valued at nearly £50,000.

Cabrera's eldest daughter, Maria Teresa Luisa (the Spanish influence can be seen in the names of the children) grew up to marry the descendant of an Italian nobleman who had first settled in England over two hundred years earlier; he was the Duke Gandolfi, who had half a dozen other titles and almost as many knight grand crosses of noble orders.

The marshal's son-in-law, who lived at the Villa Gandolfi in San Remo when he was not in residence at his English country seat at Blackmore Park, Worcester, was a deputy lieutenant for the counties of Worcester and Hereford and an active magistrate. He was a distinguished heraldist and genealogist, and had written several booklets in English and

Italian on these subjects. He also had the distinction of being the author of one of the few original English contributions to the Cabrera literature, although by any standard it is minute. In 1889 he published from Blackmore Park a four-page note on his father-in-law, over the initials T.C.G.H., Thomas Charles Gandolfi-Hornyold. (Hornyold was the old royalist family an earlier Gandolfi had married into; the Hornyolds in the mid seventeenth century had backed the Stuarts in their disastrous battles against the parliamentarians, and had forfeited their estates. They got back their lands at the Restoration. When Cabrera's grandson, the Duke Alfonso Otho, put the estate on the market in 1919 it consisted of 3250 acres, with mansions, farm houses and cottages, and took a team of auctioneers working in relays three days to bring in the proceeds of more than £100,000.)

T.C.G.H. had his note privately printed and publicly circulated, and it is bound both as preface and prologue into the duke's own gold-blocked and gold-edged copy of Don Dámaso Calbo y Rochina's illustrated history of Cabrera and the civil war, which Gandolfi-Hornyold presented to the National Library and is now in the British Museum. It has the title *Note to the Several Lives of Marshal Cabrera*, intended, it seemed, solely as a corrective to the almost unanimous conclusion of historians and biographers that Cabrera was of humble birth, and not as a commment on his charmed life, as the title could well imply. It ran true to type of the duke's other literary efforts, for it was chiefly a genealogical study designed to show that Cabrera was of noble ancestry and moved in appropriate circles.

Apart from calling his father-in-law the Lion of Castile rather than Tiger of the Maestrazgo, it made no attempt to put his life into perspective. 'The true origin of Marshal Cabrera is misgiven in this work and many others,' he says in the note. The reasons for this were that he was envied by the great nobles who surrounded Don Carlos, on account of the prominence he so quickly achieved and his extraordinary success when acting independently, unfettered by the Pretender, and that the Spanish people loved to consider the Lion of Castile as one of themselves. The duke goes on to say that Marshal Cabrera had a great disregard for titles and honours other than those won by the sword, and for this reason declined an offer by King Alfonso XII to make him a duke and grandee of Spain. He accepted the military rank of marshal because, as the senior general of division of Spain, and certainly the one, together with Espartero, who had seen greatest service, he felt entitled to it. He turned down the ducal rank lest it be said that he had gained anything by his change of politics when he saw that the accession of Alfonso was necessary to prevent the ruin of Spain. Also, 'because Spain needed the money', he never drew his marshal's pay – a fact confirmed by his young aide at Wentworth, Captain (later Major) Polo de Lara, in an adulatory military memoir of 196 pages about Cabrera he wrote ten years after Cabrera's death, which was also privately printed.

The Duke Gandolfi sets out a detailed pedigree to prove that Cabrera was of noble and ancient descent both paternally and maternally. Although they were impoverished branches of once great houses, he argued, they still held leading positions in their neighbourhoods, the Cabreras for instance having a hereditary right to a canonry in Tortosa Cathedral. This was how the young Ramón came to be educated for the Church.

There is a disturbing thread of inaccuracy running through the note. For example, the duke does not get the age of his own father right, and says he was rigorously imprisoned by King Louis Philippe of France 'for more than a year', ignoring the freedom allowed Cabrera in Paris, Hyères and Lyons. He has Maria Griño's second husband Felipe dying and widowing her a second time, when there was plenty of evidence showing him in the hills and later in exile with his stepson; and he alone says that Maria then became 'Mistress of the Posts in Tortosa', going out of his way in this some-what odd note to point out that this 'lucrative office' was a coveted position 'everywhere outside England', and was a princely prerogative in the Austrian and Roman Empires.

The duke, recording the social scene, says that Cabrera was an intimate and personal friend of the Emperor Wilhelm I of Prussia and of the Empress Eugenie of France, a Spanish-born lady, and of the Emperor Napoleon III – who as the ambitious Prince Louis had pushed Cabrera out of his prison rooms in Ham. He was also a friend of the Prussian Prince Frederich Charles and Marshal Manteuffel, and went to Germany as an observer on the Prussian general staff to follow the Franco-Prussian War which broke out in 1870.

Here, then, Cabrera had a triple interest: friends on both sides and a war which had its origins in Prim's offer of the Spanish crown to Prince Leopold von Hohenzollern, France's objections, and Bismarck's determination to goad the French into action by his notorious editing of the Ems telegram. ('I did not add a single word, I only shortened it,' Bismarck protested in his memoirs!)

Cabrera saw the French overwhelmed and Napoleon III captured, leading to the declaration of the Third Republic and the disappearance of the Empress Eugenie from the Paris scene. Before this, according to the Duke Gandolfi, the marshal often went to Paris to see the Emperor and Empress. And he records that the Empress told him that she knew Cabrera well before she was married, and that in Paris he often saw her and the Emperor in the strictest privacy in the evenings, 'Cabrera coming into the Louvre palace through a back door'. She found his conversation and energy extraordinary. 'And I do believe,' the Duke quotes her as saying, 'that he had emissaries even in the smallest village in Spain. Nothing passed without his knowledge though he lived in England and several times both the Emperor and myself thought that he would at last upset the throne of my good friend, my cousin Queen Isabella.'

Isabel, after she was overthrown in 1868, came to Paris, where she had a meeting with Carlos VII on the neutral ground of a Paris boulevard and, according to the note, saw Cabrera. The Duke quotes Isabel: 'I never was so much moved in my life as when Cabrera, my arch-enemy, who had caused me so many sleepless nights, kissed my hand and said Madam, I ask you to forget the past; because I am a Spaniard, a Royalist, and a lover of our unfortunate country, I truly rejoice in the accession to the throne of your son, my King.' The Queen added: 'Though Cabrera was my worst enemy, I always esteemed him and after all, his faults were those of a Spaniard, and we all have them.'

Cabrera may well have had his spies in every part of Spain;

likewise, his own movements in England were closely watched by agents of the Spanish Government – 'at very great expense', says the Duke Gandolfi, who goes on to aver that the marshal was offered the presidency of Mexico by both the national parties there. But he declined, and supported the candidature of the Austrian Archduke Maximilian, younger brother of the Emperor Franz Josef, 'whom he visited at Miramar, near Trieste for six weeks . . . giving him advice which unfortunately was not followed'.

The duke does not disclose what this advice was. But history records that Maximilian accepted the crown of Mexico, and after three years as a very troubled emperor was court-martialled and executed by Mexican nationalists when in 1867 French troops were withdrawn under Marshal Bazaine – the same Bazaine who as a young captain had taken over command of the French Foreign Legion when its commander, Conrad, was killed by the Carlists at the battle of Barbastro thirty years earlier.

The Duke Gandolfi died in San Remo in 1906; his body was brought back to England by the duchess, Cabrera's daughter, and interred in the Hornyold-Gandolfi vault in the Church of Our Blessed Lady, Blackmore Park. No member of the Cabrera family apart from the duchess attended the funeral. Her own death at the British Hospital in Paris, twelve years later, was reported in the local paper amid columns of casualties of the First World War; her body was brought back to Blackmore Park after the war to lie beside the duke. They left two sons and a daughter, the Countess Charlotte, but the Gandolfi title has now faded into disuse, the present lineal descendant choosing to be known as plain 'Mr'.

The marshal's first son, Ramón, married and had a son, handing down the titles Conde de Morella, Marquis del Ter, which continue to this day. The third son, Leopold, was apparently a social misfit, and was packed off to Australia with a few shillings in his pocket. Leopold made little of his life there. He returned to England and, broken in mind, died at the age of forty-nine. He is buried at the Roman Catholic church of St Edward the Confessor, Windsor, built in 1868 largely through the generosity of his father, who bought the land and guaranteed building costs. A mass is still celebrated for Cabrera every year on 24 May, the anniversary of his death, and Leopold is commemorated in stained glass windows in the sanctuary.

The youngest daughter seemed to inherit her father's determination if not his sentiments. When she was born at Wentworth in 1863, the marshal's influence could have been waning, for unlike the other children she was given an English name, Ada.

The marriage of the ruthless Carlist commander and the equally strong-willed Protestant lady seems, nevertheless, to have been happy; or perhaps his forceful personality may have been sufficient to maintain a façade of family unity. But when the old tiger died, the tigress took over, and was apparently as ruthless on the hearth as he had been on the battlefield. For a deep division split the family asunder; Ada and her mother, entrenched at Wentworth, on one side, and the three boys and the Duchess Gandolfi on the other. According to the Countess Charlotte, Cabrera's granddaughter, talking to the author at her home at Sunningdale, Berkshire before she died there in 1979 in her ninety-second year, the prime cause was religious. Although Marianne had known full well what she was doing when she married a Catholic, she remained an ardent Protestant and became increasingly unhappy as the Catholic Church took hold of her sons and daughters. However, she held on to Ada, her youngest, and brought her up as a Protestant despite the fact that the girl was baptized a Catholic. It could also have been that the Spanish influence and thinking of the father, domineering and ruthless as it must have been given his make-up and experiences, had purchased the minds and character of his sons and first daughter; and that Marianne, the great county lady, and Ada, the daughter with the plain English name, outraged and goaded by this, had reacted to become more English than ever – stolid English conservatism and Protestantism clashing with Spanish anarchism and Catholicism – so that when the master departed they decided to cut themselves off from it for ever.

Ramón Cabrera died a year after the Carlist wars in Spain had finally ended, comforted again by the last rites of the Catholic Church and in the presence of his two aides, Colonel

'The village church, the railed-off square' – Cabrera's tomb at Virginia Water, England.

Llanos and Captain Polo, and of the Spanish minister in London.

Hundreds of people from the Virginia Water, Egham and Chertsey areas went to his funeral and saw the man they knew only as their respected squire and patriarch buried in the railed-off corner of the churchyard at Christ Church, a corner formed from land carved out of the Wentworth estate. The countess was attended by the Spanish Minister and members of his entourage, and followed by her three sons. The British Army was represented by General Whitmore of the Horse Guards and by General Spence, the Navy by Captain Byng. On a coffin of polished oak rested the marshal's baton, sword and cocked hat. The inscription read:

> *Field Marshal Ramón Cabrera, Count de Morella, Marquis del Ter, died May 24th 1877, in the seventy-first year of his age.*

Although in the happy licence of the report of his wedding, the *Illustrated London News* had referred to him as 'the gallant general', the Surrey local paper had no such compliment when reporting the death of his bride sixty-five years later. 'The Carlist desperado' was the blunt description; and the local paper went on to venture a tally of his victims: 1100 prisoners of war shot by him, it said, without (one assumes) going into the civilian count.

His death renewed the differences that had divided writers on Cabrera in the 1840s. Then, as far as the Cristinos and their propagandists were concerned, he had become an enemy general, and therefore had to be damned. Now the Carlists were damning him themselves, for in their eyes he had become a traitor to the cause. In London, the former correspondent on horseback Charles Lewis Gruneisen recalled Cabrera's dash and fury outside Madrid, in a letter published in the *Pall Mall Gazette* and intended as a counterblast to articles in other newspapers looking back on Cabrera's life, raking over his barbaric acts and retelling stories true and untrue. For instance, the *Echo*, the *Gazette's* rival among London evening papers, had said that of all the hideous brood engendered by the guerrilla revolutions of Spain, 'no one was more blackly stained with blood, more depraved by cruelty, or more degraded by treason', so much so that his own townsmen, the burghers of Tortosa, had blotted out his name from their list of citizens. It recalled that when he came to London 'men shunned him and fathers forbade their daughters to dance with him or even to touch his hand – and yet he affected all the airs of gallantry and fashion and actually won the heart and hand of an English girl who was a heiress'.

Gruneisen, the ageing war correspondent, summing up the old general he had ridden with all the way to Madrid in the days of their youth, would have none of this. His letter, full of misinformation about Cabrera's early days and why and how he had joined the Carlists (which could conceivably have been implanted by Cabrera himself), showed how pro-Carlist and pro-Cabrera he remained. He described Cabrera as a kindly and humane gentleman, whether in Spain or in his later life in England, and 'always a patriot'; that was why, in his closing years, he came to desert the Carlist cause, an act that, Gruneisen said, shocked him as much as anyone – yet he understood it.

Gruneisen's was almost a lone voice in the London press, although *The Times* conceded that Cabrera had changed during his life in England. He was one of those men, it said, who are brought to the surface by revolution or civil war, who show wonderful aptitude for command in lawless times, and with the coming of peace are crushed into tameness by the weight of social conventions. His long residence in England had opened his eyes to the folly of the Carlist enterprise. Having married an English lady, and settled down to the life of a prosperous country gentleman, he had put aside the wild notions of his guerrilla days, and had lost all resemblance to the ruthless chief who had left so many dark memories of himself in Spain – a man who had gained complete ascendancy over his followers, and kept it by shooting with his own hand any of his soldiers who showed the slightest insubordination. Conspicuous even in that ruthless war for his cruelty, the only excuse for him was that both sides shot prisoners of war in cold blood, and he was terribly provoked by the execution of his mother.

19

Family Feud . . .
The £300,000 Will

If Cabrera had brought any gold out of Spain he had used it in the cause, for his estate amounted to less than £4000. He bequeathed everything to his widow, who chose to carry on his title as the dowager countess. She was then fifty-six; and having ridden the tiger for nearly thirty years, she rode a horse for another thirty; she followed hounds till she was over eighty, and only stopped when she fell off her horse and broke a leg.

The quarrel with all her children except Ada was bitter, and when, in the last years of her life, her eldest son, himself now the Count of Morella, came to England with his wife and son, she had Wentworth barricaded. Detectives and uniformed police guarded the house, and her workers patrolled the grounds. The count, who was in the Spanish diplomatic service and lived in Madrid, had had his letters to his mother returned, and came to Wentworth in the summer of 1913 to try to establish communications. They put up at the Wheatsheaf Hotel and sent the young man into Wentworth, not exactly under a white flag but nevertheless as an emissary of peace, carrying a letter. The son, also named Ramón, a lieutenant in the Spanish army, managed to break through the cordon and reach a window of the great house, from which his grandmother shouted: 'Go away, man, I do not wish to see you!' He tried again the next day, and she had him thrown out of the grounds. A policeman spotted him and blew his whistle; one of the estate employees seized him by the scruff of the neck, another by the back of his coat, and they frog-marched him down the drive and out of the gates, threatening to duck him in the pond.

155

Ramon had three of his grandmother's employees up for assault before the Chertsey magistrates. In evidence, he said his only desire was to deliver the letter personally. He claimed he did not believe the orders to keep him out came from his grandmother; he thought he was being kept from her. When she told him to leave she had not known he was her grandson. Another officer of the Spanish army, a Captain Edmundo O'Ryan, said he saw Ramón hustled out of the Wentworth gates; he was not struggling but going quietly. The defendants disputed this, and one said that Ramón had struck him in the chest. Their defence, that they were acting under their employer's instructions and that Mr Cabrera was an undoubted trespasser, was accepted, and the case dismissed. Neither the dowager countess nor her daughter Ada attended, although the estate agent gave evidence of receiving their instructions to keep the Cabreras out.

Ramón was then twenty-four. As his military career progressed, he came into contact with another young officer three years or so his junior, by name Francisco Franco. They both fought through the Riff War in the 1920s, when the Moroccan nationalist leader Abd-el-Krim challenged first the might of Spain, then that of France, before yielding to a combined assault of the two – a campaign that saw Franco leave his comrade-in-arms far behind to rise from major to brigadier-general and become the youngest general in Europe. When the civil war that was to translate Francisco Franco to the helm of the Spanish state broke out some ten years later Ramón Cabrera the third, who was a British subject by birth, went out to join him and became his confidential agent in Tangier. Cabrera died soon afterwards, the victim of a motor accident while taking despatches to Ceuta in January 1938. There were some odd factors about the crash, and as some factions were known to be hostile to him and he was also probably on the Republican black list, there was talk that his car had been sabotaged, and that he was murdered.

Marianne Catherine was only six years short of her century when she died at Wentworth on 16 April 1915. The local paper, in recording the misdeeds of her 'desperado' husband and recalling the Wentworth fracas, had kindlier things to say of the dowager countess. 'She was so generous,' the report of her death said, 'that for years she ruled as the greatest benefactor in the district and there is no doubt that she will be sadly missed by the poor in the vicinity of Virginia Water.' The rich must have missed her, too, for it was the Garth Hounds she was following when she had the fall that fractured her thigh! And so must the local children, for they would no longer be able to enjoy their impish prank of diving into the bushes as her coach approached in order to avoid the curtsies she demanded.

Whatever the secret turmoils of their family life, she chose to lie beside her husband in the little churchyard at Virginia Water. The vault was opened up and the entrance lined with ivy and white flowers; both coffins were on view to the villagers after the mourners had departed. There were carriageloads of flowers, and nine carriages of mourners; these were led by Ada, followed by important local residents, among them Sir Charles Walpole, Chairman of the Chertsey Bench, who had been a chief justice and attorney-general in colonial territories; a famous soldier, Lieut-General Sir Edward Hutton, former ADC to the sovereign, and just home from command of the 21st Division of the Third Army on the Western Front; and a representative of Prince Christian. Then came the entire Wentworth household; at the rear her own personal carriage, empty and with blinds drawn, was followed by her farm labourers. And in spite of the Wentworth rebuff, the eldest son and the new countess were there, hopeful, perhaps, of a mention in the old lady's will. But not a whisper!

She left over £300,000, and cut out of her will all her children except Ada. She bequeathed £500 to her bailiff, £300 to her gardener and £50 to her stud groom; a year's wages to her coachman and all her indoor servants, with a suit of mourning for each. Lodgekeepers, gamekeepers, stable boys, farm labourers and other servants got just the suit.

An annuity of £100, and all her clothes, was willed to her lady's maid, Mary Brown; but she had not lived to benefit, and a lesser cross marks her proper station outside the Cabrera enclosure at Christ Church, as another opposite marks the rank of the marshal's aide, Major Luis Polo, who lived on at Wentworth twenty-five years after his master. Her solicitor received £500 and her doctor £200. The residue, worth about £¼ million, went 'to Ada, my youngest daughter'.

Not a mention of the three sons or her duchess daughter. The only reference to Spanish connections came in four annuities. The marshal's two aides-de-camp received them, as did two Spanish ladies, Maria and Bienvenida Cabrera, both of Tortosa, described as 'sisters of my late husband'. The first received an annuity of £100, the other of £50.

Not even the proverbial shilling for the heir presumptive, the present count. No mention of Leopold or Ferdinand. Nothing for Maria Teresa. In fact, in a codicil dated 5 May 1911, Marianne Catherine specifically willed that if Ada should predecease her, the residue of the estate should go outside the family, to a Camberley officer, Colonel Johnston Stonehouse Talbot, absolutely; and if he died, to his son.

When Ada sought to prove the will the count contested it. The case came before Mr Justice Bargrave Deane in the Probate and Registry Division of the High Court. Count Ramón did not appear, but solicitors representing him applied for the will to be set aside. The case seemed to revolve around the 5 May codicil, which as Ada had survived her mother no longer applied. The codicil had been found in a sealed envelope with instructions that it be destroyed. This had not been done, and it was opened on the judge's order. Ada had engaged four counsel, led by Sir Edward Carson, KC; the count had none. Marianne had made the will twenty-five years earlier, and the judge asked her solicitor: 'Was she of sound mind?' 'Undoubtedly,' he replied. Formal evidence was given of the proper execution of the will and of its codicils, the Wentworth butler, William Cosham, testifying to the execution of the 5 May addition – the one showing that she was determined to keep her money from the Spanish Cabreras. The count's solicitors withdrew all opposition, and Mr Justice Deane pronounced in favour of the will and all its codicils.

The favoured daughter continued to live at Wentworth for some time before the estate was sold. She then moved to Englefield Green, and then to Guildford. She died there, at

Cantavieja . . . the Tiger's lair, the Wentworth cottage.

Hill House, Hervey Road, on 1 May 1934, aged seventy-one.

She had never married, and her passing made few headlines, although her estate was still worth £¼ million. She had received something like this amount from her mother, and picked up another £50,000 from brother Ferdinand, the Kaiser's master of ceremonies. His estate had been proved to the public trustee in London when he died in Berlin without making a will. Ada, four years after his death and three years after her mother's, applied to Mr Justice Horridge in the Probate Division, and had the administration of the estate revoked completely in her favour.

Ada's will ran to seventeen foolscap pages. She left £1000 to each of her three executors – her doctor, Harold Gabb of Guildford, and two Kent solicitors, Alexander and Ronald Brett; £600 cash, the income from a £20,000 trust fund and all her jewellery to her woman companion, Agnes l'Oste Probart. £2000 went to a London dockland priest; £50 to the vicar of Egham; £10,000 to the Bishop of London's Fund; £10,000 to the Royal National Lifeboat Institution; £5000 to Alexander Brett in addition to his legacy as an executor 'in appreciation of all he did for me in a difficult time of my life' – most likely a reference to the family feud, and in particular the Wentworth skirmish. The Society for the Propagation of the Gospel received £10,000; a year's wages went to each of her servants; and the residue to the National Benevolent Institution. Not one bequest to anyone or anything of Spanish origin. Ada eschewed the family tomb and left instructions that she be buried wherever she might die – in the event the cemetery at Stoughton, near Guildford. There was just one hint that there had ever been anything Spanish in the family; among the small bequests an annuity was given to George and Katie Stroud, of Cantavieja Cottage, on the Wentworth estate. Cantavieja! The Tiger's lair in the mountains of Aragon! It is the only mark of the father to be found anywhere in his daughter's will.

Cantavieja Cottage, near the Cabrera enclosure at Christ Church, stands to this day. So do Tortosa, Ebro, Cabrera and 'elter' Cottages, all marked with the Morella crown – the last named a monument, also, to a stonemason obviously better at his craft than he was at reading, for his chisel translated the Spanish title *el Ter* into a little gem of English nonsense. Not far away the names Cabrera Avenue and Cabrera Close, in a latter-day housing estate, also recall his presence. Over at Wentworth the putters click on greens laid where Carlist kings and plotters used to tread, while in the big house talk is of lesser battles lost and won.

The congregations at Christ Church cannot escape Ramón Cabrera either, for on the wall of the south transept a massive corniched plaque in white marble commemorates him and Marianne Catherine, his wife. Nearby, Major Luis Polo, his faithful aide, remains for ever on guard, remembered with the text 'for whom the Lord loveth He chasteneth'! And in the railed-off vault in the shaded corner of the churchyard, where the sun strikes through the trees to gild the weathered cross, the man himself lies. With him his lady, who despite everything set these plaques in the churchyard wall behind the cross before she joined him for ever:

> To *the beloved memory of Ramón Cabrera*
> *the Valiant General of Carlos V and Carlos VI.*
>
> *There the wicked cease from troubling, and there*
> *the weary be at rest.*

Bibliography

de Arjona, Emilio. *Pages d'histoire du partie Carliste, Charles VII et Ramón Cabrera.* Paris, 1875
Aronson, Theo. *Royal Vendetta.* London, 1966
Ayguals de Izco, Wenceslao. *Tigre del Maestrazgo.* Madrid, 1849
Bertrand, Louis. *Histoire d'Espagne.* Paris, 1932
Berrow's Worcester Journal
Blackwood's Magazine
Borkenau, Dr Franz. *The Spanish Cockpit.* London, 1937
Borrow, George. *The Bible in Spain.* London, 1843
Brenan, Gerald. *The Spanish Labyrinth.* London, 1943
Cabello, F., Santa Cruz, F., Temprado, R. M. *Historia de la Guerra Ultima en Aragon y Valencia.* Madrid, 1845–6
Cabrera, Los Montemolinistas y Republicanos en Cataluna. Madrid 1849
Calbo y Rochina de Castro, Damaso. *Historia de Cabrera y de la Guerra Civil en Aragon, Valencia, y Murcia.* Madrid, 1846
Cardigan, Countess of. *My Recollections.* London, 1909
Carr, Raymond. *Spain, 1809–1839.* London, 1966
Caso, José Indalecio. *La Cuestion Cabrera.* Madrid, 1875
Clarke, H. Butler. *Modern Spain, 1815–98.* Cambridge, 1906
Coles, S. F. A. *Franco of Spain.* London, 1955
Cordoba, Buenventura de. *Vida Militar y Politica de Cabrera.* Madrid, 1844–5
D'Auvergne, Edmund B. *Queen at Bay.* London, 1910
Duncan, Francis. *The English in Spain.* London, 1877
The Echo
El Caudillo de Morella [Poems]. Madrid, 1849
Eliot, E. G. *Papers Relating to Lord Eliot's Mission to Spain.* Privately, 1871
Evans, Sir de Lacy. *Memoranda of the Contest in Spain.* London, 1840
Farr, Revd Thomas. *A Traveller's Rambling Reminiscences of the Spanish War.* London, 1838
Ford, Richard. *Gatherings from Spain.* London, 1846
Furley, John. *Among the Carlists.* London, 1876

The Gentleman's Magazine
Gonzalez de la Cruz, Rafael. *El Vengador y la Sombra de Cabrera.* Madrid, 1849
Gribble, Francis. *The Tragedy of Isabella II.* London, 1913
Guedalla, P. *The Two Marshals.* London, 1943
Hansard
Haverty, Martin. *Wanderings in Spain.* London, 1844
Henningsen, C. F. *Twelve Months With Zumulacárregui.* London, 1836
Hills, George. *Franco: The Man and His Nation.* London, 1967
Historia de Cabrera. Madrid, 1846
Historia de la vida, hechos de armas y principales sucesos del Carlista General Ramón Cabrera. Valladolid, 1851
Historia del General Carlista Don Ramón Cabrera. Madrid, 1880
Historia del General Don Baldomero Espartero. Madrid, 1874
Holt, Edgar. *The Carlist Wars in Spain.* London, 1967
Honan, Michael Burke. *The Court and Camp of Don Carlos.* London, 1836
Hume, Martin A. S. *Modern Spain, 1788–1898.* London, 1899
Hornyold, T. C. G. H. *Note to the Several Lives of Marshal Cabrera.* Privately, 1899
Illustrated London News
Jordan's Annual Register
Kirkpatrick, General E. de C. *Don Carlos Against Don Alfonso.* London, 1875
Latimer, Elizabeth Wormeley. *Spain in the Nineteenth Century.* Chicago, 1898
Lichnowsky, Prince F. *Souvenirs de la Guerra Civile en Espagne, 1837–39.* Paris, 1844
Livermore, Harold. *A History of Spain.* London, 1958
Men of the Time
Morning Post
Oyarzun, Roman. *Vida de Ramón Cabrera y las Guerras Carlistas.* Barcelona, 1961
Pall Mall Gazette
Poco Mas, *Scenes and Adventures in Spain from 1835 to 1840.* London, 1845
de Polnay, Peter. *A Queen of Spain.* London, 1962
Polo de Lara, Captain Don Luis. *Cabrera, First Conde de Morella, First Marquis del Ter.* Privately, 1887
Pirala, Antonio. *Historia de la Guerra Civil y de las Partidos Liberal y Carlista.* Madrid, 1855
Principe, and others. *Espartero: Su Pasado, Su Presente, Su Pouvenir.* Madrid, 1848

Rahden, Wilhelm Baron von. *Cabrera: Erinnerungen aus dem Spanischen Buregerkreige*. Frankfurt, 1840

Raikes, Thomas. *Journal*. London, 1858

Shaw, Colonel Charles. *Personal Memoirs and Correspondence*. London, 1837

Somerville, Alexander. *The British Legion in Spain*. London 1839

Surrey Herald

The Times

Tomas, Mariano. *Ramón Cabrera: Historia de un Hombre*. Barcelona, 1939.

Index

(Page numbers given in **bold** type refer to illustrations.)

167

4/84

SANTANDER
BILBAO
Guernica
SAN SEBASTIAN
Irun
Durango
Oriamendi
Dancharinea
Basque Provinces
Vergara
Ebro
PAMPLONA
VITORIA
Estella
Zuniga
Montejurra
NAVAR
Miranda de Ebro
BURGOS
LOGRONO
PALENCIA
VALLADOLID
SORIA
Douro
Almazan
ZARA
OLD CASTILE
SEGOVIA
San Ildefonso
(La Granja)
Renales
Molina
de Aragon
Brihuega
ÁVILA
GUADALAJARA
El Escorial
Alcala
de Henares
MADRID
Vallecas
Fuentiduena
CUENCA
Aranjuez
Talavera
de la Reina
Tagus
Tarancon
TOLEDO
NEW CASTILE
Guadiana
CIUDAD REAL
Granatula
ALBACETE
La Mancha